CW00406385

A State Of Independence

– Stride –

Other Stride anthologies:

Earth Ascending: an anthology of living poetry
edited by Jay Ramsay

A Curious Architecture: a selection of contemporary prose poems
edited by David Miller and Rupert Loydell

Completing The Picture: exiles, outsiders & independents
edited by William Oxley

The Rainbow's Quivering Tongue: an anthology of women's poetry
edited by Mary Plain

Things We Said Today: poems about The Beatles
edited by Phil Bowen

The Stumbling Dance: 21 poets
edited by Rupert M. Loydell

Jewels & Binoculars: fifty poets celebrate Bob Dylan
edited by Phil Bowen

How The Net Is Gripped: a selection of contemporary American poetry
edited by David Miller and Rupert Loydell

Stonechat: ten Devon poets
edited by Christopher Southgate

Ladder To The Next Floor: Stride Magazine 1-33
edited by Rupert M. Loydell
(University of Salzburg Press)

A STATE OF INDEPENDENCE

edited by

Tony Frazer

A STATE OF INDEPENDENCE
First edition 1998
© Stride 1998
All rights reserved

Selection © Tony Frazer
Introduction © Tony Frazer

Copyright of poems
© individual authors

ISBN 1 900152 27 4

Cover photo by Rupert Loydell
Cover design by Neil Annat

Published by
Stride Publications
11 Sylvan Road, Exeter,
Devon EX4 6EW
England

INVESTMENT
SOUTH WEST ARTS

Contents

Introduction

This book contains the work of 18 poets who have been active in the British Isles in recent years. Although the majority are British, the selection also includes two Irish poets, one Canadian and one Australian, all resident in Britain at various times in the recent past, as well as one expatriate Briton based in the USA. Whatever their location, all the selected poets are publishing – or have published – the majority of their work in British presses and journals.

This does not pretend to be an exhaustive survey of the poetry of the last couple of decades, and indeed some of the writers I wished to include declined to be involved. The selection covers figures who are well-known and published by major publishing houses, as well as others who will be new to the reader unless (s)he is a very attentive follower of the small-press scene in Britain. Small presses are typically independent in outlook, often provincial in location, and are invariably not regarded seriously by the cultural establishment in the capital. All of the poets here have been published at one time or another by such presses: Roy Fisher first reached a larger audience through Migrant and then the remarkable Fulcrum Press in the 1960s; Christopher Middleton – also published by Fulcrum in the late 60s – is now published by Carcanet of Manchester, a small press which "grew up". By contrast, Philip Jenkins' books have been so fugitive that they were and remain almost impossible to find.

If these poets are so worthy of attention, why is it that they are not all given the accolades accorded their more mainstream contemporaries? It may be that refusal to play the literary-political power game or not bothering to be a reviewer / reader / lecturer / biographer proves detrimental to a poetry "career" as it exists these days in Britain. Innovators of course – and some of those included here may justifiably claim that description – are always outside the canon, until such time as they are recognised as forgotten geniuses – as with Basil Bunting in Britain – or until the canon swivels about to accommodate them – as with John Ashbery in the USA (although his fecundity and intellectual playfulness still seem distrusted in Britain). No conspiracy, this, but simply the natural moves and countermoves made by political human beings, who seek comfort with their kin and the safety of their own walls rather than an exploration of the harsher country beyond.

Some of these more independent voices nonetheless break through to a kind of reluctant recognition, accompanied by puzzlement, particularly when the critical tools of the mainstream – which dominates those journals that seek to be arbiters of taste – fail to cope with the language, strategy, structure and style of the work in question: Middleton and Fisher in their different ways are cases in point – reviews of their work in mainstream journals have often shown a spectacular inability to engage it on the appropriate level, exemplified by attempts to "situate" the latter with Philip Larkin, on the dubious grounds that both demonstrate a sense of place.

The writers in this book represent no "school". They are here because I admire their work and enjoy reading it more than most that I find on the poetry shelves in bookshops and libraries these days. The unifying principles therefore – as must surely be the case in an anthology – are personal taste, likes and dislikes. I have a long-held love for singers, for shamans, for bards, for high-modernist collage and for terse lyrics à la Robert Creeley. I look for the kind of excitement that was first afforded me by Bunting's *Briggflatts*, Graham's *Nightfishing*, Snyder's *Mountains and Rivers Without End*, or by my first encounters with Robert Creeley and Gustaf Sobin. Some of the poets here I've been reading for nearly twenty-five years, others for no more than 18 months, but they all give me enjoyment, and give me pause.

There are obvious absences (some voluntary, as I have already noted), but some less obvious that may require explanation. Performance writing – a notable part of the alternative poetry scene – is not represented here, largely because I have not had the opportunity of experiencing it in performance & because I remain unconvinced by what I have seen of the printed variety. The loss is likely to be mine. Likewise, concrete poetry of any kind is unrepresented for the simple reason that its heyday would seem to have passed some time ago, notwithstanding the glorious exception of Ian Hamilton Finlay, who occupies a well-nigh unique position half way between literature and visual art.

This book could have been twice as long, and perhaps contained another dozen poets. It could also have been three or four times as long if I had decided to include anglophone poets from the USA, Canada, Australia, India and elsewhere. There is a job there for someone with large printing and permissions budgets, particularly if that someone is prepared to look beyond narrow definitions of what constitutes, or should constitute the current acceptable "canon". Anthologies in recent years have tended to be "official" or of the corrective "antidote" variety, such as this in part seeks to be: there is room for someone to draw the strands together.

Tony Frazer

GUY BIRCHARD

Coup de lance

Buddha beams at the Xtian
hearses. Señor, Lord, every
stew bum in the Strand knows
the camera aids the hand against
the eye. My God! cusses Ives
and the poet needs Nihil
Obstat, Imprimatur
I'm tied   I'd rather
have a freehold, by the
lion and hind, by Balthazar
I would. Gill on his knees
in Geneva thanks God for this
beautiful gin! Crivelli
relieves me and he and
Longinus and we all
hear the voice cry
Eli

commentary

God is the hardest to praise

Triptych

the melancholy young man sees
wildlife in terms of roadkill:
the romantic young man in transit
drives shy of the soft shoulder
but yearns: the aesthetic young
man travelling light writes long
hand ignorant of word processors

the melancholy young man and his
type sows sorrow: the romantic and
his type imagines a woman out of
the wind: he thinks he learns real
life from a grand master's canvas,
the aesthetic young man and his type,
picks out in the corners and deep in
perspective chicory in the landscape,
the magpie on the eaves

the melancholy young man reaps
pleasure footloose flushing
whitetails and coyotes upwind
so they lope or bound away —
he loves to try to tell one
raptor from another: the romantic
anticipates — he is mindful:
the aesthete distinguishes
tansy from millet, pigeon
grass from pig weed,
barley from buck
wheat among the fall
rye, the wild
oats

Shriven (Dafydd ap Gwilym's Edifeirwch)

The Poet of Fair Anyo, that be me,
dear office, I limn her.
By God, today
my mind pangs for that blessed wench,
pining is my pay;
for her golden body I'd die.
When the bow's sharp bolts have stuck,
and the bones cramp in the grave,
and the great act of life's played out,
at last the tongue is silenced.
Then, by the Trinity, lest laments
and hubbub fetter, let the Virgin
forgive me my trespasses,
Amen, and my song be sung.

Scrying

with my flayll I erne my brede

sheaves in heads and the deep
breathed dust from the threshing floor

flails. chaff in the draught
burlap nailed to spokes makes.

riddle screened winnow.

kernels throw far but the tail drops
short, whiteheads fan away. (straw for

the winter in foldyard and byre) Four-
bushel sacks!

sun through a crack and motes
measures at notches the dressing and
meals ...

Objet Trouvé: Coin

One sees the lions gesture. What
does it mean? They wave, view
halloo!

The star is a star;
the numeral, a numeral.

There is indecipherable script
and both 20th century and 14th
century dates which don't seem
to add, subtract, multiply, or

divide. And there is a king, one learns,
a Vth, the father of a IInd, whose crest
invests the piece with a value even more
singular to a lad who's found the silver
coruscating ...

Country Music

from the air the tops
of the knolls are blown pale

far away small pistols pop
their muzzles flash in the setting

sun on which we zoom
in, light catching trophy buckles

won riding the full eight
seconds in rodeos long ago

Twenty-Ninth Birthday Suite

your breasts are peaches
treeripe and lush,
lutecurve waist, hips'
classic turn, bold
on your belly's flat
world I play

tasselled silk of thighs'
stroke guides knees, mine,
invites kisses to succulent
folds, tickles to gracious
behind, back arches rippling
in wavelets to nape, long
fingers knit, palms press
shoulders' sweet roll

throat gives to lips anticipated
taste, my chin chivvies
your cheek, your nose crinkles,
temple and broad forehead,
scented soft brown curls veil
eyes' jubilant blue shine

[untitled]

every face has its looks
its wry good looks   its
lugubrious ailing eyes
its eager expression   its
steady candid gaze   its
appeal   its hostile stare
its calculating preoccupation
and its privacy   its hapless
naïveté   rigidities   and
promise   its wishful glance
and hazarded guesses   its
fatigued exasperation   and
its hard triumph   its cruelty
and its compassion and its
sympathy and savvy and its
bale and condemnation and
niggardliness   as well as
its allure and levity   its
wilfulness and sense and
severity and bated challenge
in love   as combative   its ire
and its flare and its graces
and its musing and its lush
hue   and   it's true   its lust
and its business and its
concessions   and its singularity
its pause   its light   that
revelation   its invitation
its happy passing recognition
and its careless disposition

"WHERE WE HAVE NEVER BEEN IS REAL"   *Spicer*

buried in a far
province or beyond
the borders of states
we may not enter

the north guards
the graves
or wrought iron

unmarked
sites untended
vigils unkept

no tombs defaced
nor roses placed
nor plucked

no living
granite kissed
no consecrations

no wings
no hallowed ground

the sorrow of never
seeing the graves of heroes

Orientation

the green leaches slowly from the edges of the leaves
                       I knew them when
they were so young they were
                    almost pathetic
a whole season lived beside this maple, it's
        the view
              from my 4th floor window
then you and I thought we would live here
a long time
now I cannot believe it could be
months before I lay
eyes on you once
more

some of your shoes remain in the closet
you follow your pursuits 1000 miles
more   (an independent woman)
and it'll be my turn sometime
but these days
I tend a bar a ten minute walk away and wonder
what to do with the bulk of our possessions
the phone connection's
too good
                breaks
                            my heart
to hear you so
                closesounding
        from so
far

                now only wrong
                numbers or the persistent life
                insurance salesman

                                even the mail
                fails week after week
                nothing shows in the box

(the badger is in his sett ...
others keep their distance ...)

                a chill glass,
                        tequila and
                Dubonnet, I drink to you, Cheers!

I walk out
        under the maple
                        its light brown litter
reminds me of the still green palms to the south
                        where I cannot go, bound
here for signals from you whom I'd love
to take

Behind the Lines

I can say German but I cannot speak
it. *Also*. I can read whole paragraphs
understanding only the odd word. French
tiens I say very well. French who hear me
say French have trouble believing I am not
fluent. Welsh. I do not speak Welsh, though
I have translated Welsh, medieval Welsh.
Latin I pronounce impeccably despite
having dropped it from my curriculum
at a very junior grade. *Excreta tauri etc.*
Mi tio es enfermo pero la carretera es
verde. Venezuelans have slapped their thighs
to hear me. But Spanish is a lovely tongue,
its cadences a perfectly recalled dream.
  el viento vivo como un corazón
I was Hungarian party-game champ parroting
foreign fricatives until the group gasped.
They were not disappointed, they were
amazed to understand I did not understand
one word. English, now, Canadian-American:
British girls, for my accent, have chucked
me under the chin but my words, undetectable
origins, incomprehensible intentions, dammit
my English words baffle English ears.

RICHARD CADDEL

from *Fantasia in the English Choral Tradition*

(WEARDALE SECTION)

lost in everyday deposits
of bedrock
        clouds bent in huge mass
as swirling lava long ago borne down
currents drifting
              signalling   granite sharp
in mineral air
everyday we share
             cumulus over
giant blocks of earth
rock laid down under what pressure
                    trees
nodding and turning bent down
under wind mass
heat meeting cold

& the people moving in slow giant eddies
like a great dance   like cloud spray
upon the face of the earth
               which had supported them
over the ores of the earth
               which had supported them
the people with wit and love and tiredness
and humour
       like granite
alive and moving
           under the clouds
over the face of earth

*

because there is no away to sling to
(turning radar dish over
may trees exploding blossom)

these fragments come
                  bounding
out of time
            to call to
the heat of the world
                  of which
we are part
            against loneliness
a pact held in
the need of leaves
                  to move
together
            their swell like the seas
the deeper
            downhill further and
darker and the
wilder higher reaching
                  to the sky
rejoicing

as to make it simple
                  and of sympathy
new

it is raining very hard
it is warm
the birds are   (plainly)
      loving it

whatever it is

*

dealing with   the anger of a friend
               in the cool evening
dealing with   the anger of a friend
               with a breeze lifting the treetops
               in the late twentieth century
dealing with   the anger of a friend
               and against all hate and cruelty
               when the birds have roosted

```
                  hearing my footsteps on tarmac
                  watching a cow blink
                  while the earth is being defoliated
dealing with      the anger of a friend
                  as clouds scud across the stars
dealing with      the anger of a friend
                  in the darkened room
dealing with      the anger of a friend
                  when it's still moist from rain
                  trying to help
dealing with      the anger of a friend
                  hearing a car go down the hill
                  and the grass pushing up pavements
                  streetlamps in islamic patterns
dealing with      the anger of a friend
                  as the flowers grow
```

*

dealing with a cow blink pushing up the darkened room   a car moist trying to grow   the birds lifting the tarmac as the clouds in islamic patterns   hearing my anger scud across the stars   the flowers   the century roosted late   a friend defoliated in the cool evening in the darkened room   hearing the earth blink   the grass still moist from hate   dealing with a friends cow   a car anger   blink in the moist evening   trying to help the flowers in the darkened room

hoping for a light to steer by but not touch

*

(REDESDALE SECTION)

```
lighthouse out there
                  insistent
loom seen off the land
loom
     of a city seen in the hills at night
signals over space
                  in the night
```

where you are

or striding over turf
                    the children
learning to catch things
                    and let them go
and I struggle for breath
for plant names

*

to recall
          those who are expert on apple trees
the trick being
                to love
anything
(a bonfire, a bird's tail
                    in flight)
                    to start with
a point
        to correlate with
it's important
              to make mistakes
in a way, once
              in a way
parsley
        reaching for the measure
the song wavered   recalling
                evening
            smell of parsley
thinned in late may after rain
                            turning
over and over
              air shifting over ground
violin,   skylarks wilder
                        reaching out
by the stone house
trees bent under wind
                    standing out
years   above a river
of years (memory)

in which there is no rest
                          song lapping
its banks at night
                          when the owls call
drift down like clouds
                          like rock
and we to each other calling
our wary friendship

*

there is too much
                          to want
to want to lose
                   of song (breath)
of heat   of light
                          passing wonderful
lending radiance

I am back in thought
                          in the hills
with scope
              to sing
the things I love
                     as they occur
this instant

everyday

Rigmarole: Block Quilt

for Ann

scrape the vellum   wipe the disk
ready to be anything
or sat down at stone table in frost
patchwork concerns

nearly crashed the car   surprised
by cornflower   blue splash   a character
in early morning traffic   care for you
and for small memories in lost context

not that you asked for a poem
curled asleep   insight of mountains
to place such pieces   spirall roundles ...
conical sections, circular pyramids

stem pulled into breathing   repeatedly
clarity of thought   capture of brindled ox
capture of cauldron   escapers
storming the glass castle

mind anyhow morning   backchat
in the kitchen   vegetables found
at the bottom of the sea   ready
to be anything   over and over

breaking bread with   light   patterned
memory   tight chested   air
beyond thule   thick condensed and gellied
mountain air you could bite

or how spots of persicaria do manifest
themselves between sixt and tenth ribbe
fallen long ago   we greet ourselves
from our separate thoughts

body falling into its own absence
common range   a shoe-leather handshake
recalled   lose the file
curling asleep under an old steep roof

branching off from   hanging onto
tom saying "socialism's not dead"
and a tenderness comes to it
snow on the mountain tops   driving

with a cold certainly makes me nervous
cato seemed to dote upon cabbadge
scrape the record   into the common range of
humbleness   each to its windy niche

living backwards   one of those characters
with a hand like a boot   weeding
all on the bare moorside   had been forested
merlin   bright-eyed in frost   forgotten

land foundered   wading out alone
a bog path, cottongrass-covered   rods and sails
sleepers in brushwood   a sub-marine herbal
ready to be anything   lasting to world's end

a long line flowing   bottle of wine
got broke   things left in sand
stitch   upon stitch   morning
and parting   over and over

was mad in the dark forest
since destroyed   breakfast
visible things   the song come down to us
or else forgotten or mauled or put aside

in a world when small   body falling
out of dreams   yellow   cream and
white on black   patient
rhythm of the cave   lost songs

lost upon fading into the autumn
patchwork   a fine concern for pattern
recalled   facing into the hills at dawn
vanity, feeding the winde   having no

grace of speech and so shamed
obliteration of the fact   the past
repeatedly   you could stand firm
on a grassblade   magpie words wideopen

finally and unasked-for   caring's not dead
written on the margins of sleep   speedwell
stitchwort, gentian   a distillation
eyes open and so much to learn from them

it's what remains   when the slate is wiped
just wanted to say   I love you
and all of this too   pieces laid side by side
for clarity   no easy way

of breath   no wasted effort
the songs finding themselves   curled asleep
miles away   escapers in tender
common range of visible things

SIX ENGLYNION

The Ash Tree That Bears Apples

Nennius

Glad it was so: not pushing for reasons
        or easy answers, just
    happy to walk down the path

with winter sun in our eyes and ears cold
        from wind, pushing branches
    from faces; no need for words.

Late afternoon, the world turning to night
        its last light weakening
    low in branches: bitter fruit

The Coat

Where to look for it? Frail light, far at sea,
        a land frost set as salt
    wind's temper fretting our steps

Going alone: breathing hard on the cold
        to break it, fear like a
    starbeam on the path, dark faith

Finally casting it off. Song lifting
        and going on alone
    in frost, the same and yet changed

DAVID CHALONER

Revisions

for Douglas Oliver

His attention is distracted
to a slight movement in one of the lower apertures.

When to act and when to remain inert. These are just two of the
questions we will be dealing with this evening.

The elevations are transmitters of spatial geometry. Holes to
let in the light and holes through which to enter and leave.

No art taboo and no grand gesture can eliminate the poignancy of
such devices.

Between the buildings the action is meticulously executed, all moves
perfectly synchronised.

Reason my dears, is not consulted.

There is an expression of force for which no symbol yet exists.

I was looking for something that reminded me of what I
said to you in a recent letter. Postscript to action.

Nudge a righteous citizen's sensibilities.

The street is filled with debris and daybreak. Broken glass
on the pavement mocks hysterical destruction but will not
relinquish that state.

A figure breaks from cover and runs, crouching low, into
the shadow of a doorway.

The element of surprise makes hostages of us all.

Rural Pursuits

1

The journey out
and the return.
Any moment
is what I am waiting for.
A curious regression
in time takes hold.
Simply registered,
unbearable beyond words.
Beyond words
where the persistent sense
is one of waiting,
of an interlude
hindered at last by impatience.
Where no return is mistaken
for arriving, and arriving
is only an interlude in something
of much grander scale,
that may fail exactly
as words fail to materialise
in appropriate manner.
This assumption is another strategy
composed of dissimilar events.
And so disorder preconceived
is heir to deceit.
No artifacts, remains, or tangible
evidence to produce.
History in the making.
An immaculate shift.
A shift reflected on opaque windows,
where this future will materialise
from that past,
and we breathe again, suddenly,
relieved of counter-claims,
assumptions and returns.

2.

This road. I know this road.
This road I know. This road.
Have we spoken of familiarity?
It seems familiar, it may be
a theory, could it be
an accomplishment?
Before the journey
there is a road.
There was a road. I visited long ago,
I did not return.
Some people call
this place their home.
I know these fields, these trees,
those buildings.
Some people live here, I come here
with a journey in mind.
This journey.
I know this journey.
This journey is familiar.
I have not been here before.
Can you tell me the way
to the next town?
Can you?

I know this road. This road
to the next town. Have I ever been here
before?
Look, that group of buildings, that hill,
this junction.
This sensation, I know this sensation.
It is being here, it is recognition,
it belongs with travelling
this road.
I know this place.
I have never been here before.
Today is the first time.
Do I know this road? Can you tell me,
can you, do you know this road?

3.

At this hour the silence.
In the suburbs an uneasy cry. Business as usual.

An owl swoops between aerials, chimneys
and shadows. Business as usual.
Fear paces a room. Business as usual.
Familiar artifacts furnish the emptiness.

If you listen, it is the commonplace
shifting around, that prevents sleep.
Silence colliding softly
with its echo.
The shapely ears on a tilted head,
listening in to the relentless waves
of sounds.

Mist on the hill is hooked
to its surface by dwarf oaks,
rock outcrops and coarse grasses.
The house with the white gate,
with the shrubbery and the stream
at the end of the sloping lawn,
settles for the evening
in a pink and lurid glow.

It is so far away, the clicking
of locks and window catches
can not be heard.
It is so far away, the voices,
what they say, how they sound,
and when they speak, and when they are silent,
and when they speak again,
can not be heard.

At this hour, where you have gone
comes to the same place,
and something that did not happen once,
long ago, does not happen now, here.

When you arrive, they have moved on,
any moment now,
to where you are.

4.

He was driving and it was dark.
He was driving in the darkness of winter,
towards the house. Lights were visible
over the hedges, beyond the fields,
in the distance, in the darkness,
in the winter darkness.
The sky was blue-black, flickering
with starlight. He was driving and
it was dark, and for a moment, for one shadowy
moment, illuminated by dial-light,
it was another time, another occasion,
travelling the same road.
It was another time on this same road.
A hand reached into the car, reached in
from the darkness, from the winter darkness,
reached into his body, reached through
flesh, muscle, blood and tissue.
A savage hand that gripped the organs
resting there, that gripped and released and
pulled away. That bruised, released
and drew back, retreating into a deeper shadow
swiftly passing. A shadow of nausea,
a concentration of pain and darkness.
A winter darkness through which he was driving,
towards the lights. The lights at the base-line
of the sky. Towards the lights, coldly,
steadily, glowing.
Towards the cold glowing lights
in the darkness.

Further Instructions

for Peter Riley

From nothing. For nothing prepares a path
more pathological than loam, than darkness.
True earth. What lies. What lies in wait is the lie
of the land, crowned in copper light. Light sloping
over a ridge pulled free, pulled from free air.
Resolve. Resolve never to repeat, return.
Resolve never to return. To retrace. Never to retrace.
The lie of the land. Lost light. Last rays, slipping.
Slipping to overcast. As though to return but not
here. As though to depart, but another place.
As though arrive, but without announcement. As though
from nowhere. From where loam and darkness conjoin.
It is something and nothing prepares. For nothing.
To arrive. Depart. Retrace.
Resolve never. To repeat return but not here.
For nothing prepares for lies. For life. To act.
To act upon the moments discourse. Discovery. Resolve
response. The world outlines its utterness.
Utterance to circumscribe the world's unqualified
lineaments. To state discovery as its journey.
As though return bore likeness but not familiarity.
To repeat. For nothing. For nothing but the ability
to confront. Slipping light.
The instrument of response through knowledge.
As though another place. Here. As though controlling
divine fragments in unlimited resolve. As though
thought. Ascendant spatial matrix of engagements.
Thought, response, the instrument.
Vast expanse. Language and silence. Confrontation.
Luminous planes buckle urgently.

3 Poems from *THE EDGE*

Foreword

In memory's wilderness
Alphabet of beast tracks
Marks the empty road
Neutral curiosity invents
Questions of procedure
Tentative footsteps traverse
Remote Asiatic plains
The caravans of spice merchants
Welcome us expecting trade
Offering hospitality
Plumes of delirious dust impregnate
The material woven in cunning dreams
Fertile pastures relinquished to fallow
Land economics confound
The transient labour force
Whose trade is erased
Farms surrendered to ruin
Signify audacious outposts of failure
Erosion wounds exposed through ground cover
Reveal their millstone grit
And glacial junk united
Beneath a tangled shawl of barren excess
Low cloud delivers fine rain
Anointing Three Shires Head
Upper Swineseye, Red Brook, Spittle House
The six terraced cottages of Varden Town
Elms and pylons stoutly attending
The vacant quarters
Where fields obtrude at Fitton Town
In the garden of the local coal merchant
And preacher a rampant lilac spreads
Like an unedited anecdote
From fear that disruption might weaken
The earth's crust
To expose a yawning pit
Damnation's door, Hell's lobby
The demon profile of studded leather cowl

Transferred ranting to the pulpit
The Dipping Stone, Yearns Low, Cold Arbour
Orpheus from the underworld
Duane Eddy in the yellow light of late summer
Where fields reaped clean
Surrender their fecundity
Desires lie mutilated
Running dark and wanton
In extremis

•

At the time of your departure
You exchange the burden of silent judgment
For familiar absence
Mount the old black Raleigh
And pedal away
Spokes of glistening light fragmented
By black boots turning
Coat tied with string and grey trilby
Stained around the band
Intense morning light tilted over
Your passing form head and shoulders
Above the laid hawthorn
A silhouette of eager geometry transformed
By the brilliant wash of late september sun
Negotiations remained unresolved
In homage to the retreat from false calm
In this act of departure
All movement is stunned by silence
That bears the rebuke of laden stares
Guilt festers at the heart
Quilted cloud barricades the blue
All manner of natural and artificial
Representations clamour to be heard
Wings beat arms encircle absence
And rage clots to mucus on bloodless lips
A terrible constriction a contamination
Of dialogue set free into a songless terrain
Lip reading the names of ancient sources
And future requirements
That they might materialise to claim their due
Chanting persistently against time's clamour

•

Wherever you settle contradicts
The evidence of a self-deluding quest
Take this chronicle this exploration
This act of recall
Addressing continuity
In previous examinations of forgetting
A linear constant insists
In spite of resistance
Self control ratifies the proposal
That liberates future procession
The temperature slips a degree or two
Without guide lines without pretence
Numbed by an alien regime
Modifications are unquestionably malign
Secondary after-image of your presence
Advances intact abdicating control
Direct current to present tense
Past reactions to the whole truth in time of peril
As summer night deletes another cumbersome day
And the chambered region of your mind takes heart
And comes to understand genetic influence
Mapped onto the subject's primary response
Thoughts pivot across the earth's curve
Systematically exposed to a revelation of words
That beset preconception and its implied understanding
Of benign contempt yoked to symptoms
And complexities of desire expressed
A flag of extreme celebration salutes
Such niggardly rebuke twitching through air's entanglements
Death's fix cavorts with fractured dialogue
Bleached raiments hiss as you pass
As you turn a corner and the lush meadows
Deploy their hideous green laced with vetch
Host to an extreme celebration of flora
Glistening rush of boundless light
Where recurrent images laden with truth
Continually move away
Tracking the flawed course of unnatural lineage

PETER DENT

Naming Nothing

The micro-measure

finds

no change

in change

The endless

pause

of snowflake

into air

*

The fool's words
true, none found
but hard
to find

The burr
that catches
down untravelled
paths

*

Towing light,
a small wave
ripples
from the fog

Beam
of the eye,
to see how
light goes out

*

Falling now
the cry
but the gull
is gone

High cliff
of the mind
to hold
the song

*

Things
of the mind,
we put upon
ourselves

Each day
a garland,
endless dreams
of dust

*

To hear

inside

the falling wave

a silence

Naming nothing,

hear it

fill

with noise

*

Brightness

trickles

from the hour,

the pebbles fall

Gift

of the tide

re-satisfies

the tide

*

Cascade
of light,
the wren
unseen

Arrested,
every note
takes leave
of time

*

Darkness
in the bell,
to steal
another hour

Alert,
a silence
waits
to break

*

Black branch
and ice, only
a word
will flower

New colours
lifted,
every Summer
feeds the well

*

Waves parallel
the land,
a slow heave
underfoot

Night sets
the world
adrift, day
brings it home

*

Now and before,

one

stepping-stone

to tread

Safe ground,

no fissure

left unstopped

by moss

*

Another light,

October

leaves the mind

a space

New cold,

the bee's

a shadow

in the ruined flowers

*

Dream interrupts
the day,
four windows
crazed with frost

Still point
the night,
a wake
of ruffled hours

*

Streets under
falling snow,
the page
goes cold

Words shelter
where they can,
first footsteps
on their own

*

Rock splinters

under light

and wind,

the chapters swell

Tears at the end,

somewhere

a dark sole

crushing dew

*

from *Place to Place*

Black cones falling
Out of night

The fine geometry
Of thoughts

We think askew
It's Autumn

Not a bruise
And everything come clear

***

No shelter here
What's said is open

To the flood of night
And yet this crosswind

History so sound
At finding by mistake

Speak on
Frail vessel go

***

Still not quite
Forgotten elms

We make our way toward
Light failing

Till we see them close
The first time   Nights

And leaves and knowing
Who we are that fall

***

Were we to move
Just so

About the world
Harvester

How few the places
We would have

To leave long legs
Our name

***

Fragrant forest air
We breathe

Who steal away
A home   Dark panels

Joist and beam
A staircase up and out

To wonder starlit
At the world that pulls

***

Such tales
They tell   The old

How time was stilled
With darkness

Lifted stones   A circle
Words would never leave

Alone make
Light their dance

ANDREW DUNCAN

Literacy

Carthage
Polis of sea-Bedouin
Seven hundred thousand souls
Behind the screens of Syrtis, the shifting sea-dune,
Graveyard of ships above the lost city:
The bay was once a plain.

Carthage
Laid out on axes according to the stars
Ruled by the council of the rich;
Foam-droplet of Sidon, the city of glass;
Entrepôt of the Western seas, thief of the alphabet;
City of capital. City made of tablets:
Calculation, interest, accounts of debt.
Did your warehouses burn for seventeen days?

Bringer of letters to the Western savages;
Ruler of Sardinia, Libya, Spain, Malta;
Of bale-depots at Tartessus; of loans
To the native chieftains; of wharves
And mining concessions on the Tin Isles.
Did the sons of the Syrian earth, the bed of Attis,
Plough the freighted seas and hazy landfalls
To the Cassiterides?
Did Sheba furnish them her rich scents?
Was there none left in the sacked city
To scratch the scabs of remelted gold?

Reduced one last time to a commodity,
The city marches off as slaves. The State
Redeems its War Loans. Capital
Is human subjugation. In the market
Slaves jump and frolic
To show their health,
Airs upon a dexterous stick.

Near the ruins
The Berbers graze their flocks,
Using clumsy clan-signs
To mark their sheep upon the flank,
Their women on the chin.

Now the desert of sand
Reaches towards the desert of signs. In the burnt treasury
Or the house of archives, the tablets remain.
They are stylized pictures, nicks for limits;
Cadmean clay of the Recording Angel.

Aleph. The bull's head no more dipped in water-flowers
Multiplies across the plain of unfired clay.
The cow is money and its calf, yearly interest.
The images in the yeast of the brain have turned to stone.
The tallies of symbolic flow
Are the figuration of an empty space.

Beth, house. The Prince is in his palace.
God is in his temple, the high mountain
Or the heart of the serf. The slave is in his barrack.

Daleth. The door which opens once and closes once
On nothing.
The nomad's tent of years
On the plain of milk, the shepherd's course,
Before the silver cord is loosed.

Lamda. The yoke.
The captive is yoked to the mill of the world.
His nerves are the belts sheaved round the little wheels,
Straps compass his forehead.
He walks
The stones will not move.
He walks
The stones will not move.
He walks
The traces slip under his prickling skin,
They hitch to his bones and his ideas.
He walks

The blood darkens his skin.
The stones stir
With a terrifying glacial roar.
It is the anvil-bone, shaking in his ear.
He walks
The quern-rod,
The world-tree, the spine's lurching pillar, starts up.
He walks. He rests by walking.
He does not move. Earth and sky move.
Time starts. The world-mill turns. Where the null was,
Pours out a world of forms.
In the storage-pit
Are all the stars of a winter night, flour
Thick as the soil of the fields,
Enough for daily bread till August.
He stops.
Everything goes quiet. The world has stopped.

Reph, man. The peasant scraping in the mud
Pauses in the heat of noon.
The serfs entered in the Temple Rolls
Know no rest. The baked mud
Has valid power upon the demarcated fields;
So many bushels per acre
Scored in my cuneiform.
We exchange symbols for corn; three fifths
Of the harvest. Such is literacy.
The dark-headed folk
Ask for talismans, scrolls
Charged with the magic Word.

Tav, the brandmark. The caress of iron.
The symbol which holds. The binder.
The technical enhancement of the skin.

Teth, theta. The sun-wheel.
The gold of wedding-rings and the red of dawn's rim,
The lifted lid of the furnace, the swooped triumphal arch.
The lord of the twelve-spoked chariot
With the coachwork of gold
With the axles of light

Races the upper plain.
A turret of steep metal
Weighs on the furrows of the earth.
The dark-headed people stoop in the fire of noon.

The villages produce corn: we produce tablets.
Sheaving stone, impropriated harvests.
The corn is waggoned in. The towns swell like archives,
Baked mud coding the tilled plain.
Assessments mar the peasant's heart like stones.

We squat for years and scrutinize the tablets,
Our gaze trapped in the interstices of the plates.
Bureaucratic class
Serfs of fat and rote memories
Oppressors of all that would deploy in passion,
We are the numbers of the lord's dreams.
We quake and turn like cheese,
Arrestors of the impulse before the threshold,
Processing the numbest of all delusions ...

Almond Wind: formal lament for Osip Mandelstam

A wind blew in the region of the Black Sea.
It was like the outcry of a bird.
It carried enough almond blossom
To hide the surface of a lake.
It blew
A note so pure it drank the enthralled air
And drifted on the European shore.
Where it ruffled
A face formed in the water.

The rain-bearing wind cast down a lake.
The lake has a triple form:
The choppy lake, turned to a fish's cold and broken skin;
The lake given by the night an endless starry depth;
The lake firm and bright as glass
Which frees the eye and accedes to the total blue.

As in the stressed languages the steps of ictus —
Pinions, spirit hammers, quivers along the cord of air —
Ascend from height to height of lifting breath
In the tiers of stress, so
The superlative draws the mind;
As a slope draws water across the broken horizons of earth.
Through the pitches of matter.
The lake forms the image of an almond tree.

A word was spoken
In that stellar black;
A rhythm crossed the inner span of darkness.
Matter shook itself like dust on a cymbal,
Mountains froze along the globe's chords,
And a green wind raised trees from clay and light.
Then rocks and trees moved at man's command,
And all sang to greet the rising sun.

When the Thracians tore him limb from limb
The sun died with Orpheus,
Space turned to division as his motion ceased,
The sap of the flowers perished with his fluids
And measure was parted by his dismembered language.
A generation of spectres caught up his phrase.
The poisonous yew ate up the white and fluttering birch,
And the birch sleeps frozen in the cask of yew.
Drilled masses shook the earth, marching to song,
The ash-shafts struck roots and estates in the slatted sky:
Spear-leaves, a forest of hammered sun, shimmered.
Scythians paused on the mountain hinge between sea and sea,
Cast wooden lots upon a painted drum,
And moved out onto the plain to found States.

Now, snow cuts the tongues of rivers, pierces the fruit's flesh:
And the snow takes up the buried shapes like Reason.
Thralls work the seigneurial furrows,
And a warrior caste reaps and winnows peoples.
When he unleashed the screams we still hear
The true sound of trees and water died
And the sun was darkened by corrupted sight.
Madness slurslurs the rhythm of words to bestiality,

And the work-gang's drum beats without grace or tremor,
The mountain man stands in the middle of Saint Petersburg,
And the sycophant rhymes slaughterhouse with altar.

Where the wind ruffles the pool
A face forms in the water. I mimic it,
Worship it, disperse it, ask it questions.
How should I arrange my days? My thoughts?
Thoughts die, each leaves a seed, a part
Of the measure. The safety of the plant
Is in the rhythm, pouring in its pulsing rest;
What men cut into glass or write on linen
Or what strophes the wind recites.
Because what's said can never be silenced
We part from each word to replete the measure.
Oh voice inside,
The image-bearing stream between light and the dark fastness,
Which scales, shoots, sprays; is steeped and tinged and
Driven by great swept-axis blades.
What days come to us
When that voice is once untuned?

Mother and father bequeath little but breath;
Their air carried to a far land.
Unskimmed by angels, we still hear
It beating around our heads. By lakes at sunrise;
As agonists in love; in
Discussion by night;
We glimpse the true and sheafing Spring, the green wind.

A pure wind wafts the white flurries;
Its scansion is higher than the rigorous stave.
Snow falls on your bare head as you turn away,
An old Jew thinly dressed among the work-gang.
A wind blew over the shores of the Black Sea.

The June Sun Cast as the Absent Lover

The embrace of the sun strips me and lays me out,
The warm clasp sliding across my skin
Is not corporeal and not affectionate.
Reckless and remote,
A shock of gold unshackles my limbs.
Nothing is so warm except blood.

I know your blood is strong, o sun, it fattens
In a million grapes and wells upon the tendril
And gleams red when it is spilt; it rears like a beast
In the glass enclosure; its Syrahs and Tokays,
Its muscats and Monemvasias,
Its tears and hazes,
Its flocs and drowses,
Irrigate your body.
I drink your cognac, o sun, I
Drink your Lombard blossoms in a fragrant grove,
I drink your Franconian wine in lacquer bowls,
I replace my bleak blood with yours.
Your limbs are all of grapes, my sun;
Your skin is the sea flashing in the shallows.
I drink your summers, spirits, sugars;
I pass out in your milk of splendour.

Up there the Fall is still happening, the
Fragments of Paradise fall incessantly to the ground,
The wounded darkness loosens its clench,
Eden's unnamed florescence thrives for a threemonth.

Dark lines crackle your ingot, I see
Your face shaped, my love; I see your smile,
I know you for a second. Who are you?
Your compassion turns up my face where I live
In the sad darks.
Your beauty drops my eyes, your beauty
May I not sustain. Am I not pious?
Do I not wait for you? The berry
Is white unripened in the late season,
And I waited in vain for the sun.

You cause the skin to cry out loud, you repeal
The blindness of the limbs, they form images
In bright mass on their lolling pulp.
I lie here in the grass and listen
To the shapes stirring written across my body.

In the evening is repentance, the white
Petals of regret fall from the cooling sky,
The images of the day drift as memories into the North;
In the Morning
Is labour, the back bent in harness,
The iron across the forge; the straight light
Envelops the curved edges of machines like a Zeiss lens,
There is neither memory nor fatigue.
Those are good hours.
Noon is the hour of love,
It beats like a bell in the heavens;
Noon is the shaft of love, the star flares
Cracking open on the blue hull of steel,
The zenith and arrogance of the day,
Its hunger, its flanks of meat, its gold cuirass
Strapping gold limbs, its animals lowering
Their heads to drink; its
Wet blazes trickling out over the grass, the weight
Of mid-day pressing me down, softening my limbs.

I ripen myself in the torrent of golden drops,
Reaped in the Fields of the Blessed, ropes
Of flax and linen hailing in motes and silence.
The sunshine is swallows ripened on a tree,
And the swallows are sunlight fledged and fletched,
Cutting the fabric of the fine beamness.

I lucify myself with immensity and
Drench myself in density and
Glaze myself with gaudy gold and
Fleece myself with plumes of stellar velocity.

At Cumae

(Cumae 1987)

Whatever I know is carried away on the breeze
Blowing from the heart of the rock, where the wells
Of light are cut into the cold hill.
Sibyl of a hundred voices, what is my fate?
Sibilate
Whatever places whatever bodies
Whatever pleasures and whatever longings
Will be mine

The blue lash's drift of susurration
Lifts besides yours. Sea of winejars sheet of copper
Sea of chance! That medium
In which men fall like dice through air
Or drugs through flesh
Borne up and pinned down
Washed through the strophes of an unmoved voice;

And by the edge, at its warmest and filthiest,
Where heads swim at the gulls' diving-place
Sailors consult the women of the harbours
Salt skin chapped in the frayed sparrage and cords of the night;
Behind the wharves, the red stews and daubes,
Campanian wines with a putrid edge
Divide the days of exile
And the women foretell love and voyages,
The cold bony jaws of fish,
Seeing too far into the patterns of the flesh.

I am uncertain, crone who looks out from stone lip,
Whether I will ever possess human flesh again,
Knowing it with the rule of my hands
Tugging it into position and vanishing in that place
As vessels burst in my head like strong wine
Driving the blood in lashings against the skin
Rearing welts and engorgements on a white drape.
Tell me, tell me true

Has my soul left my body and lost its way
Lingering on the sumptuous torn fruits of the South
Or the whorled unreadable tracks of the Northern darkness
On whose rim the sun's drops freeze as amber?

The forces lock till awareness is lost.
Ships ventured too far into the hatred of the stars
Warm bodies lapped in the cold mineral blood
Crawling in the shallows where the water shines like tin
Heartbeat fading in the reckonable tide

I have foreseen too much. My fate is blank;
The breezes blur and hiss a hundred syllables,
Run through the many holes in the cliff
Modulating and delaying
As if a throat's curve in living rock
Spoke words
In a primitive language
Before knowledge and from where the waters come,
The heart caught on air as if a face on a mirror
Lifted out of the broken surface of the self
Where an eye might see many moments as flashes, paused
To turn motion into shape.

I hear parts of many sounds
Perhaps the surf, perhaps my blood beating or
A message. A heap of fragments.
What do you want. What do you want.

Wind and Wear in Aix-en-Provence

A worn part of the sky has been dismantled.
The coping-stone from the tower in the Knights' Church,
Flanking the gutter where the celestial waters drained,
Was winched down and laid here in the yard: worn
(Soft golden flesh) by the centuries on guard;
Pitted, sodden, blown, gnawn, rubbed;
Rewarded with shape for its lack of resistance.

The raspberry on the earth-trailing branch
Lifts to reveal the moth: a cluster
Of fruits impaired and pierced, half lost
Half transformed into the robber, wings draggled,
Sleeping in black veils under the red riches.

And me, soaked and soluble,
Where experience's jags
Fret the pure quadrilaterals of omnipotence,
I am replete and steeped. Pattern
Is the ruins of time; and time is feasting on us.

Flakes of transience glint
Words like fruit, light likenesses scattered
Over fairways. To speak is to wear the air,
To impart to the soft pouring medium all falling
Shapes. A wind pours steadily from the Alps and
Is part of their being; the mountain
With its scarf of air
Is contoured by abrasion. The
Universe is edible; the universe eats
Living stone to dessert on airy men.

Beside the channel where waters pour
The boundary is overwashed on both sides;
Breached on a micro scale; pores distend its skin
As if the fluids of sensation lapped at it.
Edges impart to pulp a contour.
Too many sides or too few.
Coloured scales leafwise on a counterpane.

The Torch Bearer who opens the lid of dawn
Inverts his Torch to close the rim of day;
The glinting crown of Presence, bright sickle,
Strip of transformance, THE THIN REFRACTOR
Objects double
To cross that bound, possessed and eaten up
Only to change the body which
Perceives, clasping within eyes or jaws,
So wraps an outside and breaks it,
Into error and vanity and self.

The gaze mounted on a moving arm flicks through momentary horizons
Turrets spray a pulse of light.
The mind is a boundary, sickle wing
Dragged through objects as they flash by
They are sopped up and sullied in my mouth,
A splash of vapour both into illusion and forgetting.

Those colours would be impossible without my eyes,
Part of the plan of fruit-trees;
Without the mammal eye, no coloured fruit;
A lure for clever simians, fed by the tree
To broad-cast its pips all amain across.
The tree memorized my longings long ago,
Expecting sun nitrates and monkeys. Midway
Between the absolute transience of light
And the sonority of massive stone,
The flickering solidity of animates.
Dappled in being. Forests wander.
The sun's edge is not up there,
But deep within the earth, where the living surface ends;
I stretch my edge
Out on visible radiance to where the fruits are.
I get close to the universe by eating it.

Every pattern is wear and erosion.
Each one is completed by the scanner's death.
Moth and wind have gained their shares in me,
Each line of division lets fluids pass.
Sounds may fly when my carcass dies,
The apple is falling when it starts its flight.

ROY FISHER

Near Garmsley Camp

Under great heat we're searching
the slopes above Kyre brook
for antiquities: earthwork banks,
moats, mounds. There's a need
between us to discover something.

We're in a strange descent; curving
through a young plantation, aspens
or white poplars, spaced leaves
on straight pale poles, stage trees,
a wood.
      Beyond that, the track
baffles, turns into nothing or anything;

but best, at the bottom of the wood
a field-gate chained shut
and an unmarked meadow, thickly
hedged round, and floating above itself,
floating a foot above its own grassy floor
as a silky, flushed
level of seed-heads, lifted
on invisible stalks and barely
ruffling; a surface cloudy and soft enough
to turn the daylight;
           except where
close at hand you and I can
stare sidelong through it and down
into the measurable depth of clear air
and watch winged creatures swim
high and low through the stems.

Thus far down, and seeming
further; translucent patch set into
what seems the opaque ground. Above,
the bright opaque haze of the afternoon

has hilltop trees, towers, telegraph poles
rising into it as if into infinite
distance;
      but visible for miles
a man stands sunlit and hammering
high on Edvyn Loach church steeple,
trespassing in the air claimed for spirits
by the stone push upwards, and giving
the game away; an entire man standing
upright in the sky.

The Burning Graves at Netherton

This is a hill that holds the church up.

This is a hill that burned
part of itself away:

down in the coal measures
a slow smoulder

breaking out idly at last
high on the slope

in patches
among the churchyard avenues.

Netherton church lifts up
out of the falling land below Dudley;

on its clean promontory
you see it from far off.

Not burning. The fire
never raged, nor did the graves flame
even by night, the old
Black Country vision of
hell-furnaces.

A lazy desiccation. The soil first
parched, turned into sand, buckled
and sagged and split. In places
it would gape a bit, with soot
where the smoke came curling out.

And the gravestones
keeled, slid out of line,
lifted a corner, lost
a slab, surrendered
their design; caved
in. They hung their grasses
down into the smoke.

Strange graves in any case;
some of them edged
with brick, even with glazed white
urinal brick, bevelled
at the corners; glass
covers askew
on faded green and purple
plastic diadems of flowers.

Patchy collapses, unsafe ground.
No cataclysm. Rather
a loss of face, a great
untidiness and shame;

Silence. Absence. Fire.

Over the hill, in the lee,
differently troubled,
a small raw council estate
grown old. Red brick
flaky, unpointed,
the same green grass uncut
before each house.
Few people, some boarded windows,
flat cracked concrete roadways
curving round, and a purpose-built
shop like a battered command-post.

All speaking that circumstance
of prison or institution
where food and excrement are close
company. Concrete, glazed brick
for limits. A wooded hill
at its back.

Silence. Absence. Fire.

Staffordshire Red
for Geoffrey Hill

There are still clefts cut in the earth
to receive us living:

the turn in the road, sheer through
the sandstone at Offley
caught me unawares,
and drew me, car and all,
down in the rock

closed overhead with trees
that arched from the walls,
their watery green
lighting ferns and moss-shags.

I had not been looking for the passage,
only for the way;

but being suddenly in
was drawn through slowly

— altering by an age,
altering again —

and then the road dropped me
out into a small, well-wooded
valley in vacancy.
Behind me

was a nondescript cleft in the trees.
It was still the same sunless afternoon,
no north or south anywhere in the sky.
By side roads
I made my way out and round again
across the mildnesses of Staffordshire
where the world changes with every mile
and never says so.

When I came face to face with the entry
I passed myself through it a second time,
to see how it was.

It was as it had been.

The savage cut in the red ridge,
the turn in the traveller's bowels,
by design ancient or not;
the brush-flick of energy
between earth and belly;
the evenness of it. How hard
is understanding? Some things
are lying in wait in the world,
walking about in the world,
happening when touched, as they must.

Handsworth Liberties

I
Open —
and away

in all directions:
room at last for the sky
and a horizon;

for pale new towers in the north
right on the line.

It all
radiates outwards
in a lightheaded air
without image;

there is a world.
It has been made
out of the tracks of waves
broken against the rim
and coming back awry; at the final
flicker they are old grass and fences.
With special intensity
they gather and break out
through birch-bark knuckles.

2
Lazily into the curve,
two roads of similar importance
but different ages, join,

doubling the daylight
where the traffic doubles,
the spaces
where the new cut through
cleared the old buildings back
remaining clear
even when built on.

3
A thin smoke
in the air as dusk approaches;
unpointed brickwork
lightly soiled,
not new, not old;

papery pink roses
in the smoke.

The place is full of people.
It is thin. They are moving.
The windows
hold up the twilight.
It will be dark, but never deep.

4

Something has to happen here.
There must be change.
It's the place
from which the old world fell away
leaning in its dark hollow.

We can go there
into the seepage,
the cottage garden with hostas
in a chimneypot

or somewhere here
in the crowd of exchanges
we can change.

5

From here to there —
a trip between two locations
ill-conceived, raw, surreal
outgrowths of common sense, almost
merging one into the other

except for the turn
where here and there
change places, the moment
always a surprise:

on an ordinary day a brief
lightness, charm between realities;

on a good day, a break
life can flood in and fill.

6

Tranquility a manner;
peace, a quality.

With not even a whiff of peace
tranquilities ride the dusk
rank upon rank,
the light catching their edges.

Take masonry
and vegetation.
Witness composition
repeatedly.

7

The tall place
the top to it
the arena with a crowd.

They do things by the roadside
they could have done in rooms,
but think this better,

settling amid the traffic
on the central reservation turf,
the heart of everything
between the trees.

And with style: they bring
midnight and its trappings out
into the sun shadows.

8

At the end of the familiar,
throwing away the end
of the first energy, regardless;
nothing for getting home with —

if there's more
it rises from under the first
step into the strange
and under the next and goes on
lifting up all the way;

nothing has a history. The most
gnarled things are all new,

mercurial tongues
dart in at the mouth,
in at the ears;

they lick at the joints. It is new,
this moon-sweat; or by day
this walking through groundsel
among cracked concrete foundations
with devil-dung
in the corners.

Newest of all
the loading platform
of a wrecked dairy,
departure point
for a further journey
into the strangest yet —

Getting home — getting home somehow,
late, late and small.

9
Riding out of the built-up
valley without a view
on to the built-up crest
where a nondescript murky evening
comes into its own

while everybody gets home
and in under the roofs.

A place for the boys,
for the cyclists,
the strong.

10
A mild blight, a sterility,
the comfort of others'
homecoming
by way of the paved strip
down one side of the lane;

the separate streetlamps lead
through to the new houses,
which is a clear way

flanked silently
by a laundry —
brick, laurels, a cokeheap
across from the cemetery gate —
a printing works and a small
cycle factory; hard tennis courts.

The cemetery's a valley
of long grass set with marble,
separate as a sea;

apart from the pavement
asphalt and grit are spread
for floors; there are railings,
tarred. It is all
unfinished and still.

11
Hit the bottom and spread out
among towering structures
and total dirt.

The din compelling
but irrelevant
has the effect of a silence

that drowns out spirit noise
from the sunlit cumulus ranges
over the roofs.

On the way to anywhere
stop off at the old furnace —
maybe for good.

12
Travesties of the world
come out of the fog
and rest at the boundary.

They never come in:
strange vehicles,
forms of outlandish factories
carried by sound through the air,
they stop at the border,
which is no sort of place;
then they go back.

Why do they manifest themselves?
What good does watching for them do?
They come
out of a lesser world.

I shall go with them sometimes
till the journey dissolves under me.

13
Shines coldly away
down into distance
and fades
on the next rise to the mist.

If you live on a slope, the first
fact is that all
falls before anything rises,
and that can be too far away
for what it's worth. I

never went there.

Somebody else did, and
I went with them;
I didn't know why. I remember
coming a long way back
out of the hollow

where there was nothing to see
but immediacy, a long wall.

14
A falling away
                    and a rejoicing
          soon after the arrivals—
          small, bright, suspicious—
were complete:
                    strangers
sizing one another up
in front of the shade.

With the falling away
                    the tale finishes.

Before, nobody knew them,
after, there was nothing to know.
They were swept down into the sky
or let to drift along edges
that reached out, finite,
balking the advance, delaying
their disappearance out
into the clear.

15

No dark in the body
deep as this
           even though the sun
hardens the upper world.
                    A ladder
climbs down under the side
in the shadow of the tank
and crosses tarry pools.
                    There are
metals that burn the air;
a deathly blue stain
in the cinder ballast,
and out there past the shade
sunlit rust hangs on the still water.

Deep as we go
into the stink
this is not the base,
not the ground. This
is the entertainment.

16

This is where the game gets dirty.
It plays
the illusion
of insecurity.

Shops
give way to hoardings,
the ground rumbles,
the street turns to a bridge —
flare and glitter of a roadway
all wheels and feet.

There's no substance;
but inside all this
there's a summer afternoon
shining in a tired room
with a cast-iron radiator,

pipes for a gas fire:
no carpet. No motion.
No security.

HARRY GUEST

The Fifth Elegy

Airs of summer wind their way through the empty chamber
for the skulls have gone to stare behind glass at a crude
map on the museum wall. Perhaps the bones
were removed piecemeal when the mound fell in. The sun is low
and slopes of tough grass fleeced with hazel
repeat the fragrance of the day. High stone slabs
freed from burial by five thousand years of rain
stand in the light and frost. You do not like these journeys.
Along a green-sided estuary where the tides race
hedgerows are twined with dogrose and stunted
apple-trees crowd against the white-washed farmhouse.
Fuchsia blooms by the gate until late November.
Beyond the water, fields lift towards the sunset where bare rocks
are whipped by the fog. The ferry would take us dryshod
past a brown seagull floating. The brasswork shines,
flush with the fine red wood. Each screw is countersunk.
Blue leather cushions are spotless and the rowlocks
turn silently. Art matters as itself, as structure,
as joy in its own structure though the function
may be to get something across. You must remain
conscious of the surface, its music, the promise
of another world even when the devil is muttering
lacklustre words. The worst is to be tempted not to try.
Better to scoff forbidden fruit than offer
the easel for sale. You can't make money the way
you make a sonata, make a field give grain,
make love, unless the coins are counterfeit.
The unimportant aspects last each day
from nine to five. It was a still June evening.
The guests stood by the open window. When they'd gone in
to dinner, glancing round the table, she asked
my cousin where the grey lady had gone, the one
all by herself in the other room. And her host warned her
by kicking her under the table for the grey
lady was seldom seen indoors, preferring it seemed
narrow paths of the garden, the scent of stocks

and warm brown bees working among the lavender.
Old houses like churches find it hard to exclude
the bruises of memory and layers of atmosphere
placed there by prayer or perhaps incidentally
because of a quarrel never properly made up—
year after year some grudge against destiny,
letters unsealed that glowed with stale
impressions from abroad. You'll find a lace fan
and a jigsaw in that cabinet — also
a pack of cards with the nines missing. Sculling
on a foreign lake the son who'd sold the estate
heard distinctly the stable-clock chiming. There's a green
cul-de-sac lined with the graves of dogs. The hill
looks over glittering beech-trees to the moor.
You climbed a different path, one that seemed easier,
and we met by a bed of yellow roses
twisted by the wind. The children were there already
pretending to be horses. We saw the white half-moon
and the distant colours of the sea. Naturalism
is an outmoded form. For a millennium
those who were buried in the shadow of that church-tower
have known of life what we know, that reason
reaches only so far before the truth
takes over. Listen now to the first birdcall
as the trees show a barely perceptible
shiver of green. And water too is sacred in well
and trough and font like hawthorn-leaves and the red
cord that links the child to the mother. You struggled
slipping on greasy chalk in the lane that autumn
and your beauty, flushed, laughing, was such that my heart
was seized with more love than I had imagined possible.
Who though can put a face on words or claim
to interpret the sundial? All we can say for certain is
there was a house, a tomb, a copse, and beyond
the land sloped to the river-mouth. This journey
will take its place among the many ways
of identifying movement. The portraits have arrived.
So have your books. Look at the distance. It has been
a cold summer. I was told in the village this morning
that the old man who rowed the ferry has died.
We could hire a car and drive inland to the bridge.
It's not on this map but would you like to go?

Grave-Goods: Lithuania, c. 6,000 B.C.

When she was dying
they lashed her legs together.
She must not be allowed to walk.
They had all seen those who were dead
loom threatening like strangers.

A stone axe lay under her neck.
Between her knees was a bone dagger.

The boy pointed at the dagger.
When she stirred again, after the death-cold,
her fingers, groping for it through loose soil,
could cut the thongs that tied her.

The man nodded
and fetching more strips of hide
bound her wrists.
Straightening up
he spat on his hands
and cast the necklace of boar's teeth
into the pit beside her.

Hastily they scraped the earth into a pile.
Her skin seemed to flinch.
When it was all covered
they gazed at the mound in fear
Her eyes
were pressing against the dirt
striving to see them, the buriers,
those who were still alive.

Muttering words that had to be said
they backed away.

Mist hovered by the lake.
The hillock with its raw mound stood empty.
She lay there, trapped, newly dead.
The air above
quivered with curses.

High Orchids

for Lee Harwood

After the solstice, rolling winds brought rain.

The ocean tilts north,
dark under screaming seabirds.

Shadows cast by the escarpment
lengthen now.

From your study, up one floor,
you can see peonies.
Paper is stacked on the table,
with atlas, sextant,
magnifying-glass to hand.
Your books, impeccably arranged,
share space with post-cards
catalogued in boxes.
When the wind's in the south
waves are heard
rasping on shingle.
Here, you braid texts to an intricate
pattern thought up while picking your way
alert along wry
by-paths of learning where the banded
dragonfly hovers near bindweed.
Opening your mahogany
case of instruments
you gauge the exact
dimensions of a trawler
and smile, before turning your mind
to the problem of forests
in the Antipodes.

Storm-gathered, grey, the clouds approached with rain
to drench the offshore islands,
fall on to breakwater, ruffled harbour, wharf,
drum on the upturned hulls dragged above the tide,
run down sandstone cliffs grooved in the Ice Age,
glisten among names cut on the war memorial,

lash the already brimming pools and make
exotic plants waver behind streaming windows.

Beyond the spiral of the stars
waits autumn. Snow. Descent
to zero and a stagnant heart.

June now. Late June.
Below the moor
the crops are still unripe.

From my study—
three counties west of yours—
you see wooded hills
and a cathedral in winter—
also a block
of flats across half the view.
Alone on a level with bird-
flight and swaying branches
we piece words together
into something else.
At nightfall the closed
panes show us ourselves.

Rain sweeps up from the sea and obscures
the tor silhouetted on our right.
Under the spread water, grass and fern
are beaded with silver,
ironed smooth. The torrent,
in between the scrawls of foam,
glints peat-brown,
curving sleek over boulders
we once used as stepping-stones.

A thousand feet below, cars slide to the coast.
Drivers and passengers, dry,
keep in with care the air they have brought with them.
We watch the far silent road through pelting rain.
Then turn, to pass over the brow
where there will be only rock, cattle, wheatears

and heather, ponies standing with their heads down,
bracken, running water, sheep and crows.

For one week-end it's no bad thing
to walk away from wage-earning,
the old literary squabbles,
family-ties —
then leave the land of otter and hawk
to come back, bathed in rain,
take up our usual roles
and lock away till they are needed
curious specimens of leaf-
formation or feldspar
in the worn cabinet.

The air grows lighter. There are rifts of blue
above the ridge. A raptor hangs on the wind.
We crouch to eat, sheltered by granite.
A ring-ouzel watches us. We swap jokes.
The rain stops altogether.
It's twenty years since our first meeting.
What lies ahead?
Your eyes meet mine in wonder.

Beyond the swollen river
we squeeze the water out of our socks.
I tip half a gill from a boot
that got left behind when the rest of me
leaped for the bank.
A slate-blue heron
flaps lazily across empty grass.
We get out the map. Our route
seems straightforward. Upstream
the turf is wet and steep,
rock-surface slippery.
A gnarled rowan shakes off drops of rain.

At the valley-head the land begins to flatten.
A stone circle
juts on the skyline like a set of thorns.
To the east a patch of bog

is glittering in the sun.
Jumping the brook, you plod ahead.
Then turn and give a shout.

Flickering slightly in the wind,
some red,
some nearly white, some mauve,
orchids lift
fragile above their mottled lizard-leaves.

Would that our desks produced such blooms —
so unexpected, so correct —
as lovely though less perishable.

The Sorcerer's Squares or One Way to Read Paul Klee

This grid of pastel colours could be roofs,
crooked chimney-pots, high factories, pale fields beyond them —
the raw material of bricks and sunlight for a child to organise
into a lyric city set on a tidal river.
The mudflats glisten. Fishermen berth their punts among reeds.
The cry from a tower is sung in an unknown language.
Birds dart from the tiny gardens. At night there are fireworks.
Dry hills rise a little inland where tombs are cut
and when they're sealed the wind brings sand to drift over the lintel.
That bluegrey patch low down proves an enigma —
the wrong place for a glimpse of sky or smoke billowing,
not quite the correct sheen for water and anyway
even in a fairy-story ponds don't lie at an angle.
No, it must be an enormous carpet hung out to be beaten.
The prince and his bride will need to walk free of dust.
Flecks within flecks leave scope for differing views,
which is as it should be: find somewhere for hope to inhabit,
where in narrow yards between houses the grass stays clean,
where walls are painted pink or blue or primrose,
kept free of posters, free of slogans, never scrawled on,
where passers-by smile before greeting each other and where
no trace remains of a market after the trading is over.

Two Interpretations of a Piece by Grieg

I

Last spring. The one just past.
There were fine days — sun glancing off the fjord —
but snow clung on, reluctant to yield land
to those high flowers.
                              Last spring. It's summer now
and April was the tight, unnoticed bud that grew
to this expansive flaunting, an event
obliterated by its outcome. Scaffolding
gets taken down when the builder's finished
though hedges tend to hide their structure. Hard
weeks of preparation cringe unseen
behind the polished gestures on the stage.
All clumsiness forgotten, temper, fears
get cushioned by the sleek flesh of performance —
fake rant, flung hand, the skill that gains applause.

Last spring. October shrouds
the distances with mist. Leaves fall again.
They've filed away that brief success.
The set has been dismantled.
One notch more can be cut in the door-jamb.
Days that lighten change to nights
that lengthen. Chill sweeps down from the Arctic.
A dark corrals the frost and liquidates
the dormant butterflies, filming the pond
with cold. There was a time for youth, a case
for making plans. Last spring. Not now.

II

The last spring. Last of all.
There'll never be another. Earth
has had its chance. The egg is domed,
unbroken in the dry, abandoned nest.
From the valley-head, the slow
cliff of the glacier grinding nearer
crushes the green room where July
was so successfully rehearsed.
Our leading lady once

recurrent victim of a cardboard suicide
coughs her real lungs out on an iron bed.
No tangle of lighting cables, jars of stale cream,
ripped pages marked in pencil.
The hospital has three dimensions
and the surgeon
knows his lines.

The last spring. The very last
experiment of May. No daffodils
to spurt from softened soil, no thin cascade
skeined by the breeze in gusts of spray
across the rock-face. No crops,
no foliage. Low sun
fixed in the south and fading.
Grass grey and unreplenished. No
swifts to scream in a blue evening.
Long cold. Slow dying. Planet sphered by ice.
Silence. The end of things. Creation over.
The six bright days of Genesis have led
at last to this,
no further spring, no hope, no warmth again.
A white full-stop in space will mark the close.

Barsoom

the planet Mars in the John Carter
novels of Edgar Rice Burroughs

It is a world that has been left to die.
　　Cold sun probes thinning air. The last canals
　　lead from the ice-caps under ruined walls.
Mere skeletons of farms guard fields gone dry.

In arid light, waves of vermilion moss
　　break on abandoned wharves. Tall cities stare
　　from vacant windows past worn headlands where
the dead sea-bottoms roll through emptiness.

The planet is alive with echoes. Noons
   possess no shadows. Nights are parched and chill.
    An earthman stands alone, sword bared, far from
    the double towers of threatened Helium
   where Dejah Thoris the incomparable
waits patiently beneath the hurtling moons.

A Very English Art

Wet sky over the village or
watery sunlight on a rounded slope
where sheep graze untended or
overseen by one boy in a red cap
(sole touch of bright colour) or
foliage casting an unfinished jigsaw
of pale shadow on a paler abbey wall

The painter with his umbrella,
easel, brass-bound box of pigments,
has gone home now and left the scenes
to flying light, to intermittent rain.
Tucked safe in his portfolio
the green and gray of weather,
drift of smoke, an ochre aqueduct,
a winding path, meticulous
crossbars of a cottage window,
sunset beginning in a lake
dotted with indications of waterfowl,
a park at evening, groomed and opulent,
where a stag's long shadow falls on yellow grass.

Some trips abroad allowed the brush
to wrap crags in a thunderstorm,
shed midday brilliance on marble,
lift minarets above a sand-dune,
construct a vertical drama
crumpled with glaciers —
all very well but alien
when observation can begin
with what is near as well as far,

a low bridge across standing water,
blue field beyond —
a rain-washed steeple against massed cloud —
curved street with glinting cobbles —
kitchen-garden with silver
dew-points among the currant-bushes.

Art is the here and is the there,
the seen, the dreamed, the known, the longed for,
a winding path, meticulous
crossbars of a cottage window,
sunset beginning in a lake ...

LEE HARWOOD

Coat of Arms on Wall in Ancient City

Bears dance to the music, slowly, awkwardly
in the grand piazza.
A thin but sufficient chain keeps them in place.

Grotesque beasts look on,
beasts cobbled together from various spare parts
and men's strange imaginations.
Is that a crocodile or an eroded dragon?
A winged lion or a sphinx?
All the world's plunder cobbled together.

Mists coat the lagoon this evening
as the ferry passes a low barge,
a pleasure launch and a small naval landing craft
on the flat waters.

In the palazzo an evening of decadence
is about to begin and the end is expectantly planned
for systematic and cold debauchery,
whips and black undergarments,
a series of calculated and delightful humiliations,
pains and pleasures.

Has the icon, looted from Cyprus, seen it all before?
The resigned virgin with child
cluttered with necklaces and improbable crowns.
A look of indifference is all we see.
She may sternly pity our fate, or
not even know it. Tough luck!
We'll get by.

We board the throbbing steamer.
Here come the bears hurrying from their last
evening performance and just in time.

"All aboard" someone shouts in Italian.
The splendours fade behind us as
we're cloaked in a sweet velvet darkness.
Ahead is the unseen landing stage,
the sound of crickets and frogs
and a bored bus driver calling to a friend.

The bears troop off and disappear into the night.
Their plans remain ambiguous.

The Unfinished Opera

for Marian

Overture

In a remote grove in Kansas you sit
on the deck before your home.

The gramophone is wound up and through the hiss
of the old record a rich bass sings
Don Quichotte's dying words to Sancho Panza:

> "I promised you an island once,
>   now all I give you
>   is an island of dreams."

You get up from the deck and go indoors.

I walk through the long grass in my dreams
towards your grove to visit,
to even introduce this ancient gramophone
you don't possess
and play an old opera record
you may not like.

The sky reddens as dusk approaches,
a vast magnificent sky ceiling your grove
that I now enter. Name the names.

A spacious grove of walnut trees, hackberry,
elm, red elm, locust, pin oak, bur oak,
hickory, ash, and osage that now
fades into the coming night.

Leaning against a tree trunk I watch you
move from room to room.
In your lit home   out in the darkness
my face against the bark   you raise a hand to your face.

Not as a ghost or wandering spirit I come
but as a dreamer
whose love surrounds you
like the Egyptian dead that walk beside you.

The day's heat still radiates from the earth
as darkness finally overcomes the day
and a young moon appears in the sky
with Venus glittering below, the heart's pole star.

The curtain falls in dark red folds
and faded gold tassels. The orchestra pauses.

Act 1, Scene 1

The curtain rises on a grove in Kansas.
It is mid-afternoon.
The dreamer lies down in the long soft grass
beneath the trees.
He at first stares up through the leaves
into the clear blue of the sky,
but soon drifts into sleep.

Cunning stage machinery now hides the grove and dreamer
behind gauze curtains and we are transported to
a piazza in Venice,
or is this the town square of Baldwin?
No, it must be Venice, and the story begins.
The orchestra, after playing quietly during these changes,
boldly strikes up the new theme.

In this the dreamer's dream —

It is evening in the piazza. Don Evano enters leading his pet pangolin on a green ribbon. The Don, a vigorous blade, noted connoisseur and melancholic in his middle years, takes a seat at an outdoor cafe. He orders a dish of milk for the pangolin and a chilled glass of wine for himself. The whole recitative is performed in a fine baritone voice.

At the next table sits a lady clearly in a distressed state. It is Donna Corazon, a noted actress and patron of the arts. She engages him in conversation after the usual banter. He warms to the task after his initial reluctance. Donna Corazon is in love with the Duke Nuvola di Venti, a wild adventurer who has been away in the New World seeking his fortune for many years. She is also secretly in love with Don Evano. Don Evano is not sure who he is in love with.

Their conversation is interrupted by a religious procession, a military band, and a variety of street-vendors with appropriate songs.

At the end of this noisy diversion the orchestra quietens and we hear again the strains of the small café orchestra playing a simple popular ballad. Two figures now enter the piazza. It is the lovers Leopoldo and Marianna. They are engrossed in each other's company and sing a tender duet, "Love is my destiny". Marianna has the wit of a Countess Almaviva and the stunning beauty of a Marianna. Leopoldo is a somewhat paler figure. The couple are then greeted by Donna Corazon and Don Evano. They all four join to sing of the trials of love.

The piazza once again fills with people and the whole populace, it seems, join to sing of the trials of love, and yet its joys. The scene ends on a nervously buoyant note.

Act 1, Scene II

It is the next morning. The piazza is nearly deserted as Leopoldo and Marianna enter. They have just been told that they must leave Venice immediately. Marianna is to go to Spain to be married to her exceedingly rich but stupid cousin, while Leopoldo has been commanded to join the Imperial Austrian Army.

Leopoldo, a fair tenor, sings of his inconsolable grief at their parting. Death would be kinder if this were to be forever. He swears his eternal love for her.

After a long last embrace and duet Leopoldo leaves for Austria.

Marianna is left alone. She sings a faultless aria of her woes and fears, and yet the hope that one day they will be reunited.
As she finishes we have tears in our eyes.
We stand and applaud her singing,
we applaud her beauty,
we applaud the very conception of the whole opera.

Act 1 Scenes III & IV.

There are now two lengthy scenes filled with intrigue and misunderstandings. Beset by Albanian hussars on her journey Marianna is imprisoned, but escapes thanks to the machinations of Don Evano. Leopoldo near death on the battlefield is saved by the sudden ministrations of Donna Corazon. Various dwarfs and a few mythical beasts thread their way through the story here. An old crone appears warning one and all that "the path of love is like a bridge of hair over a chasm of fire."

The confusions and trials seem endless. Who is behind that locked door? Who leapt from the window as the baritone approached? Who has seemingly left with another?

As the curtain finally falls we feel totally exhausted.

Interval

Waking in the late afternoon amongst birdsong
I leave the grove,
walk towards your home.
A long dirt road comes from over the ridge.
A hawk circles then settles on a fence post,
flicks its wings, preening itself.
I'm without words to tell you...
And as I approach your dogs rush out
barking.

The dream takes me no further.
I stand for now only with memories and hopes
so intense they're near unbearable.

Your eyes glitter as we lie in the half light
in so close an embrace that
our breath and lips and limbs are one.
That one day we should walk across
this yard, talking, laughing, extending that embrace
into a fullness of days without limit.

You cross your new room — I can see this —
to place a blue and white vase
on a shelf, a picture on a wall,
to look at the treetops from your round window,
to smell the scent of new wood floors and walls.

Soon you will go downstairs,
get in your car and drive the 12 miles into town.
A cloud of dust will follow your path
on the country roads as the sun sets
in a fiery red then pink then mauve sky.
A clear crisp new moon rises,
a pure silver white awesome in its power.
I gasp at this as at our love.

Centuries ago an emperor sang
    "To the storms in my heart
      may she bring stillness".
That stillness and fullness we both seek.

People crowd in again, bells to perform
routine habits and lose sight of the heart.
The theatre too darkens and in the subsequent hush
the curtain slowly rises again.

Act 2, Scene 1

The scene once again is an early evening in the piazza, but many years later.
Donna Corazon and Don Evano walk together towards the cafe. The music is

light and lilting and reworks some of the earlier melodies.

Leopoldo enters. He has finally been released from the Austrian army due to the intercession of Donna Corazon. He is greeted joyfully by Don Evano and Donna Corazon and all three then sing of the delights of Venice and the carefree life. Don Evano sings the aria "I love to live, I live to love." But Leopoldo is immediately downcast at these words as he remembers Marianna.

Don Evano and Donna Corazon decide not to prolong his agony. The Don announces that that very evening Marianna is expected in Venice free at last.

In ecstasy Leopoldo sings:

> "Che ascolto? E ver saria?
> Celeste abrezza!
> Io dunque, in braccio all'idol mio,
> Novella vita d'amor vivrei?"

> "What do I hear? And is it true?
> Oh, heavenly rapture!
> And shall I thus, in my beloved's arms,
> Begin a happy loving life anew?"

The piazza fills with people — the chorus — who join with the three in rejoicing at Marianna's return. They sing of the virtues of harmony, of the tender and constant heart.

Marianna enters.

Suddenly I drop the curtain on this scene.
I stand in front of the red velvet, the toy theatre,
this elaborate allegory of our story.

We are face to face.
I look into your face, into your eyes,
through your eyes into that clear landscape
which is like an empty plain bathed in a warm sunlight.

I love you. I have loved you for twenty stumbling years.
No one ever in my life has that "power" you always have,
a force even greater than love
that makes me shudder at your touch,
so much more than passion.
The "perfection" and "paradise" of such moments
as your kiss brushes my lips
as we fall asleep in each other's arms
as we walk through a crowded market
as we stand together anywhere dazed and marvelling
at what is happening between us
in a miraculous daily life,
in the skies above and on the warm earth.
That the doors should be this open.. .

There are scuffling and muttering noises behind us. The curtain parts as Don
Evano and Donna Corazon and other members of the cast emerge, not
forgetting the pangolin, to protest at this selfish interruption of their perform-
ance.

We step into the wings our arms around each other.
The curtains are once again opened
and the opera continues

Brecon Cathedral

for Harry Guest

Early on a Sunday morning
        heavy frost whitening the ground
        ice crusted grass
an eggshell blue sky with stripes of pink low down
and on high a line of small rosy clouds
        strung above the small town
the boxed cathedral

A small congregation stands
        in the chill empty space then

half way through the Eucharist
          the bright sun rises
enough to light the upper half
          of the stained glass windows
                    behind the altar

that is to the east

                    I can't forget that
                    moment nor the powers there

                    * * *

But to praise God is a strange deed.
God or the gods need no praise,
only some thanks now and then
maybe,
whether a respectful nod
or wine poured on the ground.

                    * * *

The hills and mountains are oblivious
                    to all this stuff (maybe)
the heaven and hell the gods
                    in each of us

The sun melts the frost by mid-morning
but in the hills the pools are thick ice
A powder of snow on the north walls
of a bare amphitheatre of mountains
with red rust lines of scree cutting down into
the pale green and ochres of the moorland
Strong winds batter the empty tops
And the small sunlit town below
goes about its Sunday business

                    * * *

But it nags

talking to myself I know, but

with or without *the* love.

A book is held open to us
studded with words
the fingers held in blessing
A clear calm smile on His face
No nonsense
It's clear enough

clear as the mountains
clear as the light shafting through the windows

* * *

'out of the blue'
the child asks "Do you believe in God?"
To which a faltering adult answer
goes nowhere near satisfying the simple question.

*

Cwm Uchaf

In Brighton someone yells from a window
      down into the dark street and...

On the moon in a vast barren crater
      a rock very slowly crumbles into a fine dust

A fuzz of stars sweeps across the world
      partly known and unknown dark and light

across a table top across crowded grey cells
      in a fragile bone sphere cracked and shaky

tumbling down though never that elegant or controlled
      the stumbling descent through the days' maze

Jerked back by the stars the night sky
        pinning us to the ground in glad surrender

The absurd joke painful as a rock blow
        sleep though more prolonged sweeps on and over

There is a silence you can almost touch
        its pulse lick its fingers though

never complete always a faint ringing in
        the darkness

A sighing wind the noise of distant waves
        raking a seashore

All put in a box in this cave the
        star arms remote embrace

The soft fur of an animal stepping
        out of the cave two paces four paws

Then beginning to back back

Under the stars white dots drops
        of rich red blood drip onto the floor

In unknown halls bare and functional
        as a thick orange bag on a hospital trolley

The faint glitter of the rocks mica the sky
        catching the eye stood still almost

The dust the waves going nowhere in particular
        a gradual leaking away

On the Ledge

a scratched rock wall.
falling out of life
through glaring light,
no, through dark smudges,
white and grey, snow and ice,
rock. cold air. flashings.

a final thudding stillness.

your body stretched out in a snow patch
beside a long black boulder.

alone on the rock
in this silence.   I.   then
clawed ice of a continued ascent
weeping shouting alone on the rock.

and you gone silently   down
through grey winter air
the mountains we loved

PHILIP JENKINS

CAIRO

Book 1 (1978)

1.

and the darkest hour is just
before dawn   goes the song   the sound
necessarily fades

a spacious wooden floor
right angles extending out
touch the heavy curtains

the darkest segment of the film

the night
a diamond
hard tonality

a minor key   chords caused to
buoy up slowly

        the black sand
and heat of the desert

the darkest sequence

2.

what's outside this?   (her voice)
outside *this*?

the film is badly overexposed

blank empty space

(tape hiss)

3.

    I am at the centre of what I own to be a quadrilateral
Certainly   Beyond this, I can specify no further
without the appropriate instruments of measurement.

    I have used the term *centre* loosely   A world
defined by geometry   A world of meanings and
contexts.

    The proximity of forms.

4.

a wall

beyond this wall
another wall

her voice on the radio

from this land
into that

a crack appears

behind which
is plaster

behind which
is a wall

the *centre* is decayed
nothing adheres

5.

> *Water is rarely absent from any*
> *wholly satisfactory situation.*
> De Selby

It is the moist principle conditions all
genesis and generation

In the Cairo Museum, a snake
with its tail in its mouth
symbol of the cosmic ocean
the state of perpetual flux

Porphyry in *De Antro Nympharum*
identifies the solar barque leaving Memphis
                              with its departed soul
as no solid boat but the vehicle whereby they
sail on the moist

the rain which falls
in Central Africa
the snow which melts
on the hills of Abyssinia

these are the causes of the Inundation

secret of movement
a darkness in the daytime

6.

        He re-entered, visibly flustered. "Whatever you do," he reminded, "don't mention the Void. I mentioned it once but I think I got away with it."

7.

a silence that betrays credulity

(hesitation)

a kitchen shelf that is well stocked
a model of home economy

what is necessary for survival?

what remains?

8.

the film sticks in the projector
the image: a child's face out of focus

what is there of hunger that clings
to this expression? I don't know

dans l'oubli fermé par le cadre

9.

brick by brick everything
is being removed

           a suspicion I share

the seven stars that combine to form
the constellation we know as the Great Bear

a silence that belies credulity

10.

the primordial snake, Neheb-kau, 'Provider of Attributes',
holding all subsequent creation within its folds

we are here
                gods apparently and yet
our faces remain unformed

          'in the infinity
              the nothingness
              the nowhere and
              the dark'

we are the uncreated
the predistinguishable

we are the characteristics of the Abyss.

Book 2 (1980)

1.

inside his glass cube, the
endangered species sits
watching the clock. the clerks
take notes

the moist smear the thumbprint
makes on the flesh of the orchid
dull eyes observing you
through the humidity

he breathes onto the glass
the glass is 25mm triplex
it will resist a Smith and Wesson 44 magnum
(muzzle velocity 1234 ft/sec) from 3 yards

the old man motionless in his wheelchair
geometry defines his existence
thus are we lured into the
centre of the greenhouse

moisture forms sullenly on everything

2.

A man is dreaming of his death. Quietly, he appears
through the blur of faces and positions himself at the
head of the steps. The crowds part slightly to allow him
access. Deferentially, they step back isolating him. He

appears through the blur of faces. The crowds part slightly. He positions himself at the head of the steps and the breeze covers his face like cellophane. The stifled drone of voices rises and falls. He appears through the crowds who, deferentially, step back isolating him. In slow motion, he descends towards the boat which laps noiselessly at its moorings. The breeze covers his face like cellophane as he enters the boat. He lies down among the byssus and the rush mats. The boat laps noiselessly at its moorings. Above him, the pylons from which fly the flags of his victories. The boat moves slowly off into the clear waters. He lies among the byssus and the rush mats. The pylons extend into the sky at midday. The boat moves off. Above him fly the flags of his victories. His hand is allowed to fall into the cool waters of the Nile.

3.

behind the threat: the function
a steady   even   docile light

veils of paint soak in
the colour of dried blood
a tentative existence

a small commotion like
dust rising, a thin luminous mist
on a mute ironic surface

4.

In 1964, I dreamt that I was sewn into a carcass of meat hanging in a butcher's shop. Inside, I was conscious of colour moving slowly as a succession of projected slides from rich red through purples and browns into black.

In 1977 at the Vortex, Siouxsie and the Banshees
performed a song in which the protagonist mutilates
himself before impaling himself on a butcher's hook
anticipating new skin.

In the Serapeum at Sakkarah in the third century before
Christ, Asar Hapi, the Apis bull of Memphis into whom
was sewn the dead Osiris,

> Called the life of Osiris

> Animated by the soul of Osiris.

5.

the thin line ties
the neck of the bottle
to the edge of the table

the line is heavy. it bows

that small hominoidal face
brush strokes define a vigour
mark the movements that will
obscure, eventually obliterate

the passage from the fingertips
the outstretched arm
follows through

the wooden artist's model
with its minimal joints
playing a part in many tableaux

in this one, he seems
to be contemplating geometry
in the next, he has
discovered the wheel

that elegant curve
separating black from white
yin from yang

the expression on its face again
more exactly "son regard"
disappearing under successive washes

the line that can be built anew.

Montségur, August 5th, 1980.

6.

The ancient Egyptians imagined the first principle to be,
in Damascius's words: *a Darkness beyond all intellec-
tual and spiritual perception — a Thrice-unknown
Darkness.* Henry Vaughan in *The Night* would see in
God, a *deep but dazzling darkness.*

> *It is a dark cloud*
> *that illuminates the night*
> St John of the Cross.

7.

a shock in the repeated waters
this becoming unrest

stopping suddenly, he would exclaim "you
know exactly what

happens to these passengers. they descend
into emptiness."

painfully avoiding its own reflection
a broken lens   sanded fragment

8.

the Mandaeans, compulsive baptizers,
formed their communities by rivers,
by the Jordans of sublime origin

they differentiated between "living water"
          the flowing waters of the river
                              and "turbid water"
          the water of the Abyss
          original matter of the world of darkness

For there was darkness without limit in the Abyss, and Water and Spirit,
subtle intelligent with divine power being in Chaos.
                                   Hermetica

9.

Not yet awake in a bed in Balham   unfamiliar objects on
the floor   sounds I am trying to distinguish the siren of a police
car   Sunday, September the 28th, 1980.

Walking down the road in Fulham, six days before three
things which are there and not there
          the scotch egg on the pavement
                    : it is not there
          the dark creature crawling from the parked car
                    : it is not there
          the green man overtaking me, the Mayan god, Itzamna
                    : it also is not there.

In 1974 I wrote a poem which I called *A Sailor's Suit and Cap*. Two years later, it was published as a pamphlet. Two years after that, in a state of extremis, I began to live it out.

Everything happens quickly supposedly
              except: I work slowly
                 : I understand even more slowly

I found myself cut off from all contact, remaining in a North African transit stage of my own invention. In August, 1956, Bela Lugosi died believing himself to be Count Dracula.

Lying in a hospital bed in February, 1973, my muscles impaired, I cannot raise or move my arms, my legs, my head. Only my feet move, slowly from side to side.

We arrive by a despite our own efforts. Inexorably and without remorse, we shall be here.

10.

mn'

the sluice gates are open
the Reed Marshes are inundated with water

as the breast of Nephthys
nourishes with milk that is
white, light and sweet

the canals are open

the two reed-floats of heaven
are placed for Horus that he may
ferry over therewith to Ra

the twin doors of heaven are revealed
the doors of earth also.

GRACE LAKE

viola tricolor

for judith, frank and nathan mendleson-blum

the young girl taken from a trained woman,
whose poetry was mocked not as a man's,
and charged with jealousy as her inspirational motive,
was thrust into pirateer's hands
accused of purity — the south was waiting
to tighten its iron band
— lock it with another *idea* of purity
that of revolutionary command.
to train her poetry into ice
crunched by a vocular donkey
implanted with a tightrope voice
to slice up a fair country
as broad became no love
deemed wide lined prostitution
that no other ship could be manned
by open *institution*.

it was not on the news the cries for help
and might take years to strip mystique from
what gives pleasure in defining how a girl
can never be a boy in artificial reality
and not enough of a dupe to believe that
plays throughout reality move to what came first
created artificiality and much one wanted not to wish
with food to muse on others' starving
there being no books allowed at table
took to minor anti apartheid reminders
on envelopes in christmas work
and reveries upon custard
ladled out from giant vats
by pasty girls in white starched caps

a painting struck my dream the other night
within a frame of three grooved wooden white
behind a partly revealed green foliage
custard came to light as delicious paint might
which sinks and sings with natural ecstasy
crossed in no which way here there and nowhere overmuch
firm streaks of black at most odd angles.

Ordered into Quarantine

You have told me & in the telling have placed yourself above me as my
                                                                    keeper
this lacks voice positively, though your one word devastated me
I do not therefore, following you, fill in the space or watch it for,
aware of the material nature of this structural existence which has now
become a gratuitous act, falling into exercise, you annihilated me.

It is a pity that you took my body seriously, for what fears were yours
I have raced around myself like a maypole in the act of self strangulation
what a twisted girl you were you might have sighed before you popped
me into the oven having broken me over your knee like a long french loaf.

But plaited! That calmed me. Any threads in threes. Army blankets
fulfilled a purpose, or stars scratched onto a stone floor with the heels of my
                                                                    shoes
or splitting matchsticks with a pin, an economical trick, who would have
                                                                    thought
that that would have proved useful, and to remember it in a
chamber airy and unearthly light if a blue butterfly flew out I could nip
                                                                    its wing

In one bite feed on butterfly's wing by split match light & all for silence
for the lovely long life of limitless silence for nothing but wind, sun & bird
                                                                    song

language blows away

        for kim longinotto landseer

                    it's foggy and delicious
i'm in love with a chimney stack
my aversion to applying my concentration
to what is not what i want is as strong as it ever was
although i am less bothered by machinery than i am by people
who are anyway, mostly, a lot stronger than the people who are being
turfed out from their communities to make way for f.m. and b'y.
if i had an apple macintosh i could delineate the chimney stack for you.

                i could argue until the idioms vapourized.
what Does experimental mean? in terms of division of experience
                      [determinative or subjected
but was carted off. the clerk at the family court agreed. what
other than all the trappings of western civilisation do they want?
denial of the thirties. mostly. and philosan. i've returned to deserted
landscapes. i like them but children are being fictionalised into
demons and cherubim. who is going to be invited when art has been
                                [finished?

                here, as always, i was betrayed
for staying within the confines of art. i was brought a matron's cap
that i saucered out onto a southern breeze that drifted it onto a lombard's
                            [peak.
when women are amorphous and power hungry finding causes to flip over,
they have to be doing something about everything. nothing can be left
untouched. curly hair has to be washed from the brain
scraped back or razored up and stormed into airless terminals.

Sauce

1) on the message, should goodness be lost in silence. where can these go to
now they are lowered who were found to be in hell although on high
a gargoyle to a princess, one head less, facilities with trick photography
that pure separation of visuality our schools of art have been ruling
to be an eye alone and strangely wandering, did you hear?

or are you seeing something which cannot be touched to be posited
was considered supremacist. Dearest world. I am at the mercy
of one whose nature is unlike my own. And still the truth remains as
                                                              [covered
as a Beuys grand piano in a blanket with a stitched on red cross.
Such was the Tyranny of necessity which stripped me to the bone.
how it straightens to rigid duty & is marched away. whilst musicians
                                                              [play on
their consort falling, shot in the snow, playing to hold up a city with a
                                                        [tremulous bow

2) is this something uncalled for. impossible. for not bending to her will.
and what that will might state she will not level as her sanity
was impaired by birthing me who shocked her with resemblancy.
whose face was less refined in feature, her sister did agree, &
many times would take it for analysis. vile once love exhausted
a deflected comment, these features will not pass, & if they do
it will be for reasons of pity, to them both wedded. The audacity
to challenge gods. the very thought. the very word.
and many a poor poem was thrust in to squelch with the rubbish
which would take this latter day impossible to the Council tip.
because i write: the poems are not in my face that horrified you.
the very thought. the very word. to not receive the love i felt for you.
but fed me more to hate me more or love what life abhors,
a Fruit, a brainless Carnal lassitude chewing primate gristle.

Cultural

we are then when impressions are all and bitten
judged and devoid of hostile response
as insignificantly nothing amounts to nothing
nature subjected to critical sense

seated & desolate, eyes unblinking
rocking ourselves into quatrain
punished for poverty sterilized forcibly
arms dealers drive to work the same

here come the masses fed on molasses
sexually inept and incontinent
hair undressed parroting best
ironing away without irony

how dare one dare what gall moves there
to heighten with no increase in volume
a forgotten face from a distant place
an obsession with an impression

                    *

impressions cannot be built upon
if valid results are required
art does not match it cannot conform
but by retarding format

this is extant a constrained line
which circulates around thirty objects
to enter within and not join in
presages market research projects

for those who opine that brains sublime
must have travelled in proof provided
a sojourn in some stable societies
as esoteric lacks standard merit

is defined as potentially insane &
populations sub-divided
ensures prohibition of views one-sided
whatever that may mean

Silk and Wild Tulips

Afraid of my father's power the object speaks country does it concur
Entering this petrification, perforce the accident is indicative it is
A report, repeated pondering fall, a petition, a portrait I would not bear
A portrait of throated wires through blood
It is demanded of me that I die having neglected my duty.

I read of women who have been found disregarding class, the heavy book
Bearing the sombre tone, we anyway tremble whilst we are broken down.
What is love? o what is love? the tip of the tongue, a silk white dove.
that will not fight and is crushed by speculation, a sinful breast
Cleansed, the surprising lightness in weight, the emphasis returned to
Provokation, that is the dead weight, that we cannot speak until spoken to
And divided by omission are invited to attend to the traffic signals,
                                                            [obsessively
Indicating slips, don't for one second imagine that I am in the least
                                                            [oppressed.

Prussian myzi, if only i could wait for your magnesium blue to hover
stone by stone over the shark finned ground, resonations floor me
I am told that i have reinvented my history, these fakes that have
Drifted by desire rather than by noble patriotic inclination, to be told this
Frozen kiss is a parasite berry that grows and governs our merriment
That we fall to habitude unaged & are given brown cloaks for mourning
To circle the lotus that catches the tip of the dragonfly's wing
And burning it into fruition find an exhaust pipe carved in braille
The war continues to char the air with shot speech,
Theses are buried or placed on parole for comparing the language of war
                                                            [& of peace

We are old with sound of horsehair, the most beautiful poems speak to us
Yet we know they were written in the wrong country at the wrong time
When poets were forced to cross borders despite euphorbia
Unknown by date and place, the ocean resented them when uttered
A mumbled ocean slapped to make an eternally recorded impression
When we slapped the ocean the beach was too large for reality
And petty dictatorship of relative supernity returns to the bearer
that streaks green across black meadows sky scumbled blue quaternity

the reduction by not first dissolving perhaps never dissolving
what change has no time to name its causes, its reasons
for not reading paintings as though they were rule books,
Believing themselves to be needy some make a lifetime of need
That can be expected to fall by the covers of contentment
And settling that, progress through a sequence of tranquil passages
Minute squares some crossed some kissed by stars and shells
Open'd by background loss, closed by measured step,

Around the fountain the old men slept, the women deep in the heart of roses
[rouges foncés,
And the chimney sweeps wept until they discerned that their tears had
[created ink
To tell of squares of blue & finely pointed moons, silhouetted cats'
[upturned tails
Catching at the lunatics they promised the coals would glow
Memories of tail coats arranged around angel pie & a tankard of stiff
[pheasant feathers.

Eulogy

she smoothes her skirt
to show her ineffectual language
unhappy to be english speaking
to the interesting sound of spoken greek
but what could she say? this is music
in comparison to what I speak
& that is really the crux of her problem
she feels another language not this one
she is impressed. she wants to learn
these new inflections.
but will she be seized
a traitor to the nation
he sings a sentence between talking them
it goes soft, it asserts, it narrates &
faces change, animate, picking up
on each others' words
it sounds a bit italian, a bit spanish,
the girl who is with them
told me
that that was because they were speaking mediterranean.

Abschied

for Poppy Juanita Dorothy Shoshana Ruth Pascal Mercedes Mendleson

A young child cannot reply.
One does not compare.
Or crooked turn the lines
against the sunrise

By tonight I shall have lost you
because I cannot hold you
& be anything but abused
how can anyone tell of what they do not know

These great, strident images
that cannot be read for their content
Abuse stings & smarts
my daughter of the last night.

Even that then,
surrounded by deep cushions,
fitted in to a neat myth
in the endless memory
within which we are placed
beside & to each side of each other.

but what a pity
that it should mean anything
as though the autumn
did not return a spring.

your lovely honey hair
chopped up into boyhood
your back spurred
by an anomalous blast
of old poisoned rhetoric
caught from a world
rather than reflected
by art that had held us
within the sight

of a massive candelabra
that he was prowling towards
flat on his belly
costumed in foliage
unknown to botany

Rhetorical irony
meets the Master of Terms
who lends himself
to a piece of fiction.

But what could we do
You and I

You had already captured
The art of departure
Beautifully

[untitled]

She Walked where she should have stood still, stock still.
or edging slightly, morose, if not moribund and there
she stood too far from the yorkist, to be of much use
she knelt by the casement it took her ages
her legs were too long they had been part sawn off
it was cheaper than extending the length of her rest
but he waited, as only the dead could.

the day it was dull and as silent as dullness
without any breeze to lend to this nullness
numbly did old Flem bleed with a fullness
to blench oaken gall into satin and all
the works at Tyre were appointed to dress
sixteen pieces of what were the best
crimson modules, to be routed, by errantine hergest.

finja and minja were chomping on apples
not yet incorporated into the box
break time was over, short break as always,
they continued to whiten the winnings of hergest
and that is why, lambkins, to this very hour
in the even grey drab uneventful power
when your energy overbrooks the salt will go dour...

TOM LOWENSTEIN

La Tempestà's X-Ray

Gleizes, no,
        Soulages, perhaps, working his great house brush
in a war-shadow,
        consolidating, partially, the split head of
its taper,
        panels a gray canvas of the twilight's negative, and
spreads —
        like the crushed particles of some used match-heads
rubbed on
        cartridge paper— out in broad charcoally flanks
                a ragged
honeycomb of fretwork, light-charred,
        flawed with excrements
of lunar interstices
        (crumbled nightwhale jointed into vertebrae
of chiaroscuro . . .)
        It is a dull, peppery view: a montage,
at once,
        in colonnades of basalt, and husky-cubed, industrial
             contraptions
latent, half-illumined in refrigerated alcoves
        against Jacobean panelling.
For here in this monochromatic chancel
        of bi-tones, are no complicated
Grinling Gibbonses of
        trumpetwork and oak leaf scrolls
and acanthus,
        but rather, yes, there is an austere rectilinearity of conduits,
leading one
        into another nowhere,
        like the sewer blueprint for a city
of minds on the high-rise
        that have long been stopped-up,
and are still too hygienic
        to have made use of the system,

leaving it 'clean' also.
                    Here then through our round
free-flying dream of
                    cromatismo , it is the uprights and the
laterals invading —
                    a labour-force of ghostlike neolithic masons
                                                        drafted
into the Magdalenian cave sanctuaries
                              where the beasts are a-tumble
through their sacred positions:
                              weightless oxen superimposed on
or gestating in the translucent
                              wombs of ancient horses float here:
stag, deer, mastodon, rhinoceros
                              and ibex browse adrift and shudder
and gallop in the fold-bellied
                    gravity of tertiary limestone passages —
and then, just once, it appears,
                              like a visionary warning from the finger
of some ancient child cartoonist:
                              that singular
lank shaman-figure,
                    a scrawny rectangle,
rigid in trance, bird-mask
                    and clawlike erection swooned lame
against
        the rounded girth-energy of a bison
                                        who's transected
by the other straight thing,
                    and who thus relieves himself of
the bag of his entrails —
                    The machine is in action, all right:
'Man' recognising innerly
                    the perspective of his outward measurement,
his vertebral force,
                    the weakness and necessity of perpendiculars,
the ambiguity
                    of a self-made or self-styling right angle—
It was coming and it has triumphed,
                              technic uniformity
in all its dangers and loveliness

flowering in ziggurat and pyramid societies...
But then wasn't it the old Pharaonic kingdom
    which finally entrenched the vigour
of this rectilinear conceit within our cosmos?

Think of the sky's Djed-supports assembling,
the straight-backed Ibis scribe,
    the resurrection of Osiris —
            primeval stems of lotus
pushing between underworld and sunlight,
                                    rearing serpents —
I dream of warm brown silhouettes of hunters
    upright in the papyrus marshes
raising a multitude of slanting water-fowl
    into the pruinescence of that Nilotic dawn-burst.

        Yes, and I have witnessed something
of this process' evolution,
                from the sea ice, one sullen mid-February
afternoon in the Arctic:
                the village of Tikigaq in a stubble of
nineteenth-century whalebone
                        rising over the northernmost pressure-ridges
of the 68th parallel,
                like the lower mandible of a Pleistocene
fish-jaw
        meeting the half-moon's edge, as the liquified brass
                                        of the
sun's blood-fringe descended—

        The snow swept a rough cerement
over the domed
                old uninhabited *iglu* dunes
                            where everything
has had a curve in it at some point
                        (shamans rolling up
the driftwood floor planks
                    and letting them spring back again and so on) —
And then suddenly, blazing upright
                        as though to cast its spectre
over the placid rink of perfectly

level *siquliaq* (young thin ice)
stretched out
gray as the sky's anaesthetic cataract,
and
barnacled with sugar-snow on which bear tracks visible
had slurred
their seaward passage to some breathing holes —
There
stood shining and deranged
the city of the future, inland,
Tikigaq, or Tikigatchiaq ('new-Tikigaq')
in white/blue razzle
mirage substance, not trembling
as in northern summer heat haze,
but frozen on the air,
like shark-skin tinted
sheeny freezer wrapping,
storey upon storey of prefabricated office-space
and municipal housing,
arrayed in a cross-hatching of
crane necks and derricks,
the time-vandalised multiple elongation of dwellings
a vague,
run in the air meta-city
on the latitude of the Standard Oil building
in Chicago:
unusable high-wind sun-balconies
cluttered with
transport damaged condominium acccssories —
It leapt, yes,
as does Las Vegas out of a basin
in the Mohave desert at nightfall,
or Denver glazed suddenly
against the Rockies from an aircraft cabin,
and like those centres,
Tikigaq upstretching
on exchange of metals.

And scraping the slack jello
of overt appearances,
with grinding canines,

       ice and granite,
                  back, back,
    molars churning,
                   giant blue/green glacial jawbones
    masticate and thunder,

to leave detritus of Arctic trash town
on post-glaciation Adriatic:
    lead town, *Geld* town,
town of copper west of the Rockies,
    nitrate, *ashlag* and asbestos ghost town,
megaliths of spirit-ice, platonic mica-gneiss dishevelled,
    granite's incandescent sinew streaking ruined edges,
luminous diagonals, alive striations, burning fibulae and tendons,
    light-sludge, silt of darkness' inter-osseous agglutinations
severed from the cartilage and fascia, phosphorescent,
    burning in the rays' dissection,
the final earth form scoured
                       from glaciated carnage,
    chaos junketed in shafts of curfew,
hamstrung in repeated jumble of the two dimensions —

And the city in the flat plate of the pastoral
    is the blueprint — wandering platonic —
of Manhattan, Dresden, Coventry, Southampton, Mestre, West Berlin,
    contemporary London
    bel paese! — unified already .
There it is, by Jack,
    raising its vast sunless concrete ectoplasm in the brown-out,
the cold prefabricated stanchions of the future
    rearing their anticipated, sheetlike femurs,
flesh stripped in the ice masque —

And the dancing pageants
    of Detroit and Harlem
like government-bombed Druid menhirs
    tango through the twilit asphodel
in an auroral Hadean sub-storm,
    with only an attenuated flange,
bee sting of the *éclaircissement* among the cloud scrapings:

the whole sky rubble like some disastrously planned
   B.I.A-ruined Eskimo village of the late 1990s
reflected upside-down in polished sea ice catastrophe
   on televised ultraviolet microwave 'art' vision.
These are the things when the past is so violent:
   there is a kind of peace about looking into it
like a truce between the souls of materialists
   who have suddenly transcended the infrastructure —
so they imagined it — of their agon.

Thus we see dawn rising
                        on disasters that are ahead of us:
perking like an orange and brown Fanta and coffee solution
into the inverted corneal umbrella-hood of its solitary,
gazing Ruskinesque spectator who is annotating changes in
the cloud formations,
                        aware, rueful, of those spectres
that are to have arisen in the furore of the future
pluperfect, inherent as they must be in the burning molecules
of its foetus.
            The storm is in the looking
            and from looking floods out
                              knowing innocence.

      And moving down the bank of a river
            in the strange intersection
      between all this and what's to come,
            is a solitary female bather,
      who has cast aside her garment by the ruins
            and neatly steps through short thick grass
      and the dew-laden forget-me-nots
            towards the ablutions of her childhood.

Unconscious of the maelstrom
            — since without surfaces and lightning
there can be no maelstrom —
            she treads without wariness or circumspection
into her enjoyment, which is daily and usual.

Neither neoclassicism nor expressionism have yet occurred
this time, in spite of the aforesaid, all-embracing contiguity
of Armageddon: and though the shadow of our soldier hovers
like a darkly burning pre-aborted seraph across her nudity,

    still the light slides sweetly up her lower thigh
and onto her right shoulder:
    and the face, although blackened
by the very ray that lights it
    slants gracefully away from heaven,
half bent in discretion
    to the cleansing stream water
                and she's
beautiful and certain as the goddess Flora in April.

    No man covers her with his
                nor sees her body,
which is more naked in this p*entimento*
    than any fully 'revealed' nude,
such as the woman in *La Déjeuner sur l'herbe* of Manet,
    whose nakedness is partly a reflection
of the fabric of her dandies' luncheon clothing.

Here she steps
        under the paint,
into the continuous and inconclusive plunge
    of an invisible left thigh
displacing the deep stream water, and dandling
    the surface ripples with the fingers of her right hand.

How beautiful this is at secret morning,
    and so out in the open:
and yet nothing is artless or 'natural' about it
    in the way we like to think old scenes like this are beatific:

No, it is beautiful because it is both eternal
    and without context, brusquely fresh,
and still for ever covered over,
    delectably pleasant for its quietness in the mist,
                yet

perhaps almost stultifyingly routine to contemplate the
reality of, and nothing to be ooh-ed and ah-ed at for its
pastoral ingenuousness.
                         And thus I am prompted in my softness
to imagine:
          No, there is little to dislike for being ugly in
this world: only there are certain minds that somehow seek
out squalor from in the cavities of their own repression and
project this without caring. How feckless, distant seem the
city rulers!

          But now here in this skinny-dipping
                              instant
          of pure light illumined
                         air and water,
          of no-consciousness
                         and no no-consciousness,
          the grass stems bend down
                         on the paler
          green forget-me-not branches
          and the foot-blade of the bather wavers
          without spilling dew
                         or crushing out odour
          into the roscid marjoram thicket.

          It is finished as soon as it is started,
          and though in the darkest panel
             of this flat fane of monotones,
          our gypsy maid madonna,
             undressed out of flesh's luxury
          sits cramped cold
             like a spinster on a Flemish shale slide,
          her arms and legs beneath the ray gun
             a cat's cradle of half-freezing bandages of linen,
          bone sticks crossing in the livid exhumation,
             she is not of this scene:
          she's elsewhere in *Tempesta's* X-ray,
             the bather doubly alone and lovely
          in a happy calming —
             like the misprint of a spirit
          in the body of some wicked despot —

she's slipped unnoticed into our existence,
salving, if not healing our sharp longing for identities
beyond the skeleton,
because we do not, can not genuinely see her,
and may simply know of her
persistent contiguity.

*

In this X-ray of the lightning then,
Who *is* he,
what is he becoming?

Suspended in this eternity between fire and thunder,
integrated perhaps solely with his isolation,
is he naked to us therefore,
can this be all of him, and thus we see it?

Or does it work the other way perhaps: i.e. that
the very intensity of the illumination obscures him,
his outer cloth of being
constituting just a sort of murk:
the soul itself visible only in some ulterior darkness,
or at least in the imaginary, unseen light which we take
on trust from the ray-gun of a technician
on account of
its ability to throw itself clear into the bones of things,
uprooting the skeleton from the
foggy negative of its night-view?

And in our own equivalent, suffocating humidity
before the lightning flash,
in the tension of the heaven's lowered bombast,
we too cease living in the freedom of our gratuitous spaces,
the inherent difficulties of existence
multiplying themselves in our bodies:

and we become like stuffed rag dolls
that have been dunked in a tub
of some molten material like sealing wax,
and we emerge starched and tumescent with it,

glutted by a solution which has solidified
   in every vacancy there is
      between already close-packed atoms:

Thus we spend whole adult lives and marriages:
   grown stiff and dull with the accumulation of our troubles,
and so we hanker for some catastrophic release from outside,
   which is not our own responsibility,

that we may be loosened and drain free,
   and wash out the silt
which has swollen the intestinal passages of the psyche,
   however damaging and inconclusive the fleshquake.

But this moment seldom happens:
   the dark humidity of our suffering
gathers itself into a thickness
   that surrounds us without evaporating:

on the contrary, it intensifies,
   like the globular, mamilated crystalline structures
of arsenic and pyrites,
                bulging horribly inside us
   as the clouds of jade above Castelfranco bulge,
drawing to its centre
   the sharp and terrible influx of lightning,
the eternal dagger of unsatisfied illumination,
   which, held crippled in the closely burgeoned
flatulence of minerals and gases,
   like a zigzag of agate in some gloomy matrix,
breaks never in the after-thought
   or after-revelation of a thunder,
although we may wait epochs for it in asphyxiation.

Notes

La Tempestà: The painting is by Giorgione, ca. 1505. The title derives from the lightning bolt just visible above the city in the background.

The X-Ray: In 1939, an X-ray photograph revealed that the soldier is a *pentimento* of a second nude woman, poised to bathe in the river. The X-ray also exposes a background of rectilinear forms suggestive to me at the time of writing of a twentieth century city landscape. Just as the naked woman prefigures the soldier, so the pastoral is a curtain behind which our own time waits. This notion is linked to the Hindu view, in which inconceivably vast stretches of time are endlessly repeated, the 'past' thus coming before and after the present, and the latter containing both past and future in a constant process of mutual overlay. This is another, more speculative, version of samsara.

Albert Gleizes, 1881-1953, French cubist.

Pierre Soulages, b.1919, French painter of dense black-brushed abstracts.

Grinling Gibbons, 1648-1721, English decorative carver.

cromatismo: the technique of shading with colour, used by Giovanni Bellini, Giorgione and Titian.

'it is the uprights...': for some of the thought in this passage, I am indebted to S. Giedion's *The Eternal Present: The Beginnings of Art* (Princeton University Press, 1957).

shaman figure: this is one of the very few human figures in Aurignacian and Magdalenian cave art; it is in the crypt at Lascaux.

Djed supports : 'The idea of the Djed column is that it stands firmly upright — for to be upright is to be alive... When the Djed is upright it implies that life will go on in the world.' R.T. Rundle Clark, *Myth and Symbol in Ancient Egypt*, Thames and Hudson, 1959.

Tikigaq (pronounced Tik-eh-raq): an Eskimo village in northwest Alaska. Eskimos living in iglus constructed from turf, driftwood and whale-bone over the past two millenia now live here in American-style dwellings. The nineteenth century whale-bones are the ruins of the last aboriginal dwellings. A pressure ridge is a long spine of heaped sea ice, created by the movement of wind and current.

ashlag : Hebrew for potash, which is extracted from the Dead Sea.

B.I.A. : Bureau of Indian Affairs, a U.S. government agency.

Déjeuner sur l'herbe : Giorgione's *Concert champêtre* in the Louvre, was the source for this painting.

Castelfranco: Giorgione's birthplace.

CHRISTOPHER MIDDLETON

The Scroll With Bamboo and Torrent

You need not fear me. Fear for yourself.
Antigone

1

In forty-eight ideograms the poem describes it:
A triple stem of black characters to match

A single stem, bamboo, hardly bent, the leaves
Point, shrugged into clusters, three; or, splayed,

Skeletal leaves float on a shoal of east wind.
See now the wind, it whisks into leaf a shape

Surely as it carved fresh snow that Ascham saw:
The wind a wily archer knows the caprices of,

Leaves, one gust has blown them west, some beaked,
Birdlike, others the inky clusters have drunk up.

2

So far so difficult. Now for the background:
Rocks, misshapen, roundish bulk, with scant

Bamboo still sprouting, captured by a crack.
A whiteness looks to be rushing, rushing past,

A whiteness all of a sudden is a torrent;
And thanks to tiny verticals the brush touched in,

The water took on skin, a hint of volume —
Bamboo and rock, both hold their bristling ground.

3

Now in the wind again the leaves rustle,
Now again in the torrent rocks do not move.

Ten years, day after day, I have looked at it,
And notice now, only now, how it tilts, the whole

Image: the torrent slopes, a slithering mass
Of cataract thunders down into its chasm.

I wanted to hear leaves rustle, but I cannot;
Noise deafens, the chasm has quit the picture.

That bamboo stem, so thin, how can it still
Fly up so? I wonder how those sketchy rocks

For ten thousand years have stood their ground.

The characters in the corner speak their poem.
Snug in their crypt, they mean to keep a distance.

4
Freedom hatches fools, they say.
          The pivot does not wobble. Fury
Fangs a man to gnaw on self.

Passing stranger, look they say,
          And listen. Then perfect
Activity. Die hard. Endure suspense.

And ask: are those leaves mute
          When clustered, those that flit
Open-beaked, in the wind,

Do they speak out? Are those
          Mute leaves the more serene
Because a glob absorbs all feature?

Can the leaves that shriek
          To the wind as it thrills
Around them, that have knit

Into a shape the wind, be my kin?
          Now will my sisters stoop to me,
My dauntless, ancient sisters?

Recovering Dream

A feathery tip of something traced from under
The prospect, not the action, of a dream
A feathery sensation; a contour, but relieved
Of any object, grief, or ghoul,
Sprang from a source in me apart from the me
It hardly meant to be remembered by:
A windgust rumples for a wink, like that,
A furlong of the sea.

Asleep again I open an old folio:
On buckled sheets of rag paper
A sepia script, the pointy hand of John
Donne moves composing his lost inventions;
Word by word whispered across the page
Squibs to wrench the heart, tumultuous deletions,
Luminous arcades they spanned his globe,
Building up to puzzles, agonies, paradox.

The Dundaries, a light voice fluted soon, in splendor
Outshine the Quandaries; they echo
Stories of strolls in a free city,
Forty-eight fountains, holy sounds, inhabited
Houses in the air, their gardens, all
Of a spiral substance, unpoisoned,
And not satisfactorily explained so far.

The Lost Elegy

for Lars Gustafsson

Into that light of the first September days in Skåne
They walked, figures, singular in your elegy.

Into that light, a fusion of pearl and amber,
Folded around the dark rust of barn walls

The figures in your elegy walked, on the margin of
A woodland: living and dead, they walked in time,

Neither knowing the other dead or alive,
All afloat in the light of amber and pearl.

Nothing in the world more natural
Than to read of them in your book,

To know those living who went to the edge,
To know whose dead will come to meet them,

House in its field, woodland set apart,
Trees consuming the house, field a lifetime to cross —

And meeting you in the corridor I stopped
And said this was an elegy to be translated,

For the density of its matter was a delight
Which drew from living air figures to be transformed

And got them doing a dance on the threshold
Where grace and agony, house and woodland meet.

You nodded, not in the least nonplussed;
I had sketched your poem, you recognised it:

Now, finding the time, I have been combing the book
High and low, twice ten times over:

There is, believe me, no such elegy in the book,
Yet it ran to one and a half pages exactly.

As I recall the coupled lines, see the light,
Solid figures in their clothes, the house, the field,

And hear the line I did not know existed —
"Dance in the ring without fear of afterthought,"

Now can you smell the smoke from chimneys in Skåne,
Hear in a moment the voice die out?

Tauros Mountain Sketches

1

The old Turk joined his two sheep near sundown,
Sat on a tree root, spoke now and then:
Tukurruk tukurruk. The sheep spoke back,
Not as sheep to sheep but *tukurruk tukurruk,*
The right way for a sheep to speak to a man.

2

All day since dawn in the blazing sun
And hauling what he has to haul,
Logs and apricots, hay and men,
Serene when he drinks, happy trotting,
The donkey brays a bit near nightfall.
When he brays, hold on to your hat,
His heaven is near, might sweep you in.

3

There was this bird suddenly with a trill
Delineating all the apple trees,
A trill like a whisker, the whisker bird;
And after this, the high call of the muezzin,
More whisker; the tractor, whisker; the apples,
Orchard whiskers, globular and green.

4

The wrinkled cloven features of the rock
Outcrops hereabouts, and this granny's:
Tenderly she gestured beside her —
On the road shoulder, at last gasp, her sheep.
But it can't die in the boot like a hostage,
Can it? So we drove on, but granny
Who tutored sheep through misty generations,
From lamb's first leap to milking, to wool,
Each a silken pocket, full of foibles,
We left her looking back down the empty road.

5

"Life is hard, still harder when you're dumb" —
But they aren't, in one-room stone and plaster
Huts, the graceful girls, headscarf knotted right,
In clean clothes, the mother with a scalded foot,
Taking the pain. They all sweat it out, him too,
Dawn to dusk, among the white beans, baba,
Granite face, who talks a streak.

6

Where from, the slender fingers?
With a carving knife she hacks
The block of snow somebody carried
Down the mountain. Just look,
How the slender fingers dip a piece
In the mound of sugar and establish it
Between tongue and teeth. In the town,
Wintertime ... but it's far off.
Up here, we make do with snow cream.

7

Stone on stone, four walls rose
And a cupola was rounded;
A low portal pierced one wall,
So you stoop to go on in. The spring,
Five outlets in a wide
Arc (cold star), whence gushes
Crystal water still,
They housed it in a shrine, you see

Here the huge root spread:
A willow hit by lightning, long
Before we came. Before the roof caved in,
Trees all around,

Their graves in the rock, under a green hood
They heard willow speak to water,
And housed the spring, so it could dwell
In itself, as such a place might wish to.
Yes, dwell in itself.
                    Yes, them, not us.

Language Learning

Never mind the early
Imitative stages: each
Blessèd thought
Absorbing words as

Supplied, words
Macerated in
Emotion vaporous
With age, and thought

On "warm," mechanically
Roasting, itself soon
"A memory," garden
Speckled with monuments.

At three score plus,
Your word-world splits:
Things persist, the matching
Words are not quite yours.

You forget names,
Mango and Morandi;
You recite the alphabet,
Hoping memory will snag

On a splinter, but if
A name comes back it seems
To tiptoe out of nowhere,
Voiceless, random,

A reason to wonder,
Wonder if all things, all
Words together intend
An image of something else.

Then beware: catch
The fugitive, arrest
Memory by the moment,
To that slack muscle

Tone returns with art
And exercise, you can thwart
Memory's monkey tricks,
The words team up again.

But the things, have they
Forgotten where on earth
They put their words? Words
Now do not constitute them;

Or things retract their
Public names, and you,
You still profane
Their secret ones.

How then to hear them? Though
"Dialogue with a person who
Forgot the words"
May delight the sage,

Still they rattle
Ghostly chains,
Scare not the things
But you away, perhaps.

For the things at least
Look distinct,
Are done, happening, still
They float, they hurt

Something cruel: not certain
If they want back
Into their words
Or out —

The fresh adventure,
The brighter air.

DAVID MILLER

Background Music

She showed

round face yet expressive,
smiling, showed me

the room, packing-case-
slats forming exterior—
books jammed
against, achieving
in places a wall
distinct.

What,
I asked, if it should rain? The roof, she answered,
long eaves of the roof.

.

Flutter — outside.
Hands clapping.

The house. Walls.

With that noise going on
a man lies on the pavement
gasping, groping

(film).
A projection of walls.

.

Roof,
tent structure

with high points and
gentle curves.

     The voice — *glissandi*,
and contrasts of register, tempo:
      juxtapositions   acting in
a room set off
by colour then
another.

Achieving one
colour then
another

embodiment.

.

White-painted metal chairs
and white metal tables
in dull afternoon light.

Next door to the garden
in the white-painted room
a man leapt upon a chair
to give, impromptu, a lecture:
a dream of a chair,
dull, technical, dated —
sadly dated. We
sat outside —

talked secretively
about the androgynous-looking girl
opposite, in the floppy hat.

Inside, another man upset them, the beautiful
young men and women.
You are the only one, he said
in the light of eyes he couldn't see
pressed around him.

You are the only one, he said towards them
and against them
while engaged
with the animal
he kissed and licked,
and the dog licked his face, his hands,
his mouth.

You are the only one, he said
or didn't — You are the best one here,
aren't you?
and the lovely boys and girls looked on
in distaste, fascination
to make them jealous.

.

Scabbed once-white tenements
set for demolition.
Tin, wood, nailed or stacked
where doors were.

Planted
in the street's centre—
tall
rough wooden posts.
Rain. Mud.

Back of this scene, part
of it, a
hall where
scattered
people
came: became
dancers, lonely, desperately
lonely,
thrown
into shapes

in a play of lights and shadows
out of themselves, a movement

(ghostly desire).

In dream she was after all in
Singapore, telephoning
to a painter
who used batik-dyes—

connection— this was years before.

Colours,
colours of eyes   and
then buses, streets, shanty-dwellings.

Waters,   night
and colours of the eyes

open to all obscenity
and poverty—   the colours
flowing, stained through,

strongly, deeply   through

the immense surface.

.

Simplicity's table: to sit
clean-shaped metal jug
and cups, bowl of metal,
on plain table of wood.

Simple

until its death:
texture (textures)
to give planes (in
music: planes
of sound),
moving

        from exile, in
        exile: in exile a
        lake of music.

        .

Figures,   dream and waking—
different faces   yet
there is commitment

even beyond longing.

How is this true?

An abstract development —

shocking, bewildering, perhaps,
or disappointing
to the sceptical
gentleman I worked for
(running messages, copying documents),

who remembered little paintings,
charming, 'native' pictures.
This new thing, flowing colour,
disturbed. It wasn't like
the grubby,
astonishingly grubby, photos of girls
shown to you in the streets,
or the pictures which moved on the streets,
postcards which moved as you drove into the lush countryside

where poverty, labour
and alcohol daily knocked
the 'natives' out come nightfall.

This other thing wasn't recognizable.
But forget those travelled executives with weak,
wet handshakes:

elsewhere
a man with a tenor saxophone
is reshaping *All of Me*
with strength and grace;
he names it
Background Music,
it claims
my attention.

Children

1.

there was
light at the door,
the primary sign
or how the voice was,
disguised:

process of colour separation
which
brings us

the house occupied in fear of
being taken away again,
theme of *property*,
to paint the door red
and invite the night

                      breath
which begins the process,
across the park which
dips momentarily
until the voice appears

2.

the blackboards lain flat on the ground and
the figurations disrupted,

children
jump the numbers

ash on our faces and
theirs
we came here
the technique known as "jump-cutting"
(which can be distinguished from "spilling")

to achieve
the wedding celebrations

that she cooked,
in a house in her joy

(moussaka or lasagne)

3.

people merge
she is the *one* person,
moving

moving as the piano part remains
where it is

where she is, the district that
is her voice
breaking at the fountain
of her joy
the schema,
lines of varying THICKNESS

and the night sky entirely white

4.

tent-show trumpeters and circus rings
the actual world is the possible

extent
the possible world the actual
storm / thunder
and the language so funny, so ridiculous
that it is *ineffable*
soaked in the rain, trousers
rolled up

won from
a small heat
a concentration of warmth
to oppose
bodily
in the movements of the limbs

which is a change of colour

A path a lake the very breath

night fastens upon a window
twice a small path a room
you appear at the gate you follow

down the hallway where
the television's been left
on the top of the closet

amplifications *left and right*
gate-posts two slabs of stone
time deranged and revered

chill air deep blue
of conjoined sky
and lake aciculate

a writing of true
derivations the lines
are bestowed as praise

for the lovely (slender)
and good girl
who is my friend

the victim suffers
through an image
into desire or injury
and death—your face

your very breath
visible in the cold
commands me abjure
spells dissolve harm

in the *shop of nothing*
by the way of nothing

Landscape
(for Linda Bryant)

a black so chill
it numbs the eye

you favoured rocks
I spoke up
for the comfort of trees

*

in a desert landscape
these Polish lamentations
are lifted breaking
through a wash of static

cholla and prickly-pear
seen from a moving car
the soprano's voice
that sings of grief entire

a confluence unstable
that ear shapes with eye

Confrontation

1.

They have been sitting together for a long while, talking;
one of the two drinking wine without offering any and without being asked for
it.

— Do you wait as the children in the fable, their parents
away and a tiger prowling at the gate? They must sacrifice their livestock to the
tiger as others — in the same spirit — propitiate demons, waiting for release
from their ordeal.

2.

from the bus she was there
on the balcony at eye-level
but not looking at him

moss and wild strawberry
wild-rose running in a cleft
of Derbyshire limestone

the rose of Demeter
in he remembered
the cleft of her rocks

3.

— you desire to eat
the beautiful as it's
incarnate in flesh

or image — *dignity*
you say and *freedom*
lurid absurd flashes

rebelling against darkness
language caught in the
toils of your violence

4.

the path deviates to a lake
cleared he follows it he's
drawn as by the need

to give testimony he'll
write it down as it falls
as by chance her speech

falling waking in a past
impossible her young
voice its clarity

5.

— your desires coagulate
around death their residence?
with decay and stone signs

turn and see a fresco a devil
shitting into a witch's mouth
but the witch Rangda appears

the face is exposed menaced
and the Barong can only
fight Rangda to no outcome

6.

the wind lifts a line
of small red panels strung
down the building's side

when the night comes
the waters of night drink
fall asleep wake and write

and paint in broken ink
the door open and wax
dripping on the table

BILLY MILLS

from Letters from Barcelona

ONE

so much culture amongst
the dirt — the air
laden — the city selling
itself on hoard-

ings designed by Miró
to shoppers in *el corte
ingles* or the de-
formed limbs exposed

on the metro "tengo
hambre" the sign
says I have hunger
walking the streets in
the Barrio Gótico
the bread is sub-
stantiated air — ring-
ing with "butano

butano" where note
follows note in un-
expected un-
suspected order as

Santa Lucia —
clean lines after
grandiloquent saints next
door — the smell of the

sewer the smell of
the sea reminding
the desiccate river
"are only for

those who can write
a faultless fugue straight
away with no need to
correct it" attending

the dry disks of
honesty (Lunaria
biennis) in memory
as the wind an-

swers "not conspicuously"
the strings plangency
in a certain garden
held as

instigator — the plane
of a tear on the plane
of a cheek in
the widow's palace —

fingers and bow on
the strings the narrow
streets turning back
to the no longer ri-

ver the birds and flowers
their vendors in cantus
firmus — the burden
of air attend-

ed in a kind of
attenuated exile
ordering perceptions
(how many?

and their names?) we sit
on the fifth floor and
listen to pigeons
on the roof "with con-

venient notes" the litter
lays down a map
of the city as used
regathering daily

in an order of tones
the streets turn back on
themselves as we listen
to the cello,

sustaining the note
while playing gains firmness
with confidence
sustaining the move-

ment into another
quarter — attending
again the firm song
borrowed the val-

ue implied in walking
to come at last to
no conclusion no
resolution

THREE

six pot-plants on
the balcony are
Barcelona in flower
fixed by (to our

minds) inadequate
metal hoops
the city puts on
beauty to municipal

orders and we buy it
we buy the flowers
the hoops machines
for the kitchen the

streets are transposed
by fireworks observing
the changes involved
in learning the air

humid the idea
of colour of birds
returning where stone
records water

In Sant Felip Neri
"a description of
a state of language
at a given

moment" the music
is stilled but
the voices continue
the dancers inventing

tradition (sunday)
in Plaça Sant Jaume
the city as
museum or the

unswept streets these
"almost sunless alleys"
where cats meet
to gather the elements

of music a science
of the city exposing
the roots
remembering stones

in Empuries
the too-loud radio
next door "in order
to place the birth

of the Colonia
Barcino" the
rhythm and pitch
of pigeons in streets "laid

down by the romans"
this (articulate) almost
silence after
the signs written

on cardboard requiring
assistance: to think
in a different
language in lieu

of a garden "an
interesting street"
cheap music and
the poverty disguised

as aggression
"necesito una
ayuda" the sign
says "posta guapa"

as the fireworks
re-echo the city
responding the flowers
prosper or die

enquiring we
walk the streets
to come again to this
after the bin-men after

the day defined
by speech by voices
and cars in the street
the sizzle and smell of

meat from the lower
flats these intensely
proximate others
our unknown neighbours

reading Lorine Niedecker

who told her second husband
            (after they married)
"I am a poet"

                        "a what?"

                                    *

the silence
            singing

                                    *

                        the poem
                        (let us confess it)
                        is not immutable

                        nor is the river

                                    *

of flesh
            (carnelian)
bones of white quartz

                                    *

there is a river
in this city

sluggish
mud-grey
not given to flooding

carrying too much history

*

wintergreen (pipsissewa)
astringent, tonic, alterative

*

and Darwin wrote:

"I have been making
some little trifling observations
which have interested
            and perplexed me
much."

"the stony field"

the slow accretion
of detail

      things made over
reused, renewed
so that nothing is wasted

thus we will sometimes
say:

      lets cook
some extra potatoes

and fry them
      in the morning
for breakfast

"As I was led to keep in my study during many months worms in pots filled with earth, I became interested in them, and wished to learn how far they acted consciously, and how much
mental power they displayed."

      a small rosette of leaves
pulled in

to block
    or guard
the entrance

"a curious little book"

"has been received
            with almost
laughable enthusiasm"

about 400 copies remain, stored in the top of my
wardrobe, as a reminder of the quantity of error,
the error of quantity

"I was thus led to conclude that all the vegetable mould over the whole country
had passed many times through, and will again pass many times through, the
intestinal canals of worms"

                    that this work
                    done from

                    a private
                    necessity

                    should benefit
                    the totality

this detail
discovered by accident:

an old man
        bent
in his garden

to measure
the gradient

& degree
of movement

of earth
extruded

..... *the field was always called by my sons 'the stony field'. When they ran down*
the slope the stones clattered together. I remember doubting whether I should
live to see these larger flints covered with vegetable mould and turf. But the
smaller stones disappeared before many years had elapsed, as did every one
of the larger ones after a time; so that after thirty years .... a horse could gallop
over the compact turf from one end of the field to the other, and not strike a
single stone with his shoes.

       strangely
(or not so strangely)
I've begun to notice them everywhere

little vermicular structures
            of earth
and intestinal juices

       still active
this mild
            December
though normally
they burrow

to some depth
and form a chamber
where
            "one

or several worms
will pass the winter
            rolled up
into a ball"

       tonight
the moon is silent

that is
invisible

but the room
is illuminated

by an occasional
            passing
                  car

PETER RILEY

from *READER*

Egbert Street

A name becomes a heart
and maintains life.

Somewhere between loss and
gain, in that

Narrow climate
the flower succeeds

That grows now
in the garden here

A castle
against relatives.

Golden Slumbers

To have you I would bar the fields
and turn the ores into the stream

I would occupy the eyrie of my failure
far into the night night after night

Until the ancestral bones
formed a nest for my patience

In which I would sit and couple the numbers
of my life without regret

And remember with
uncertainty the world

In which we were and not, all
our loves in vain.

from *SEA WATCHES*

VIII. Seawatch

1.
Sunk in a grass hollow in the cliff, my station,
A grave green chair. The sea is blue green white,
The sea is grey and folds, the sun is split
And the clouds are a fire. Truth is never
Quite the same, its quantum cracks but
Like a three quarter moon hands down adoring stead.

2.
Which is a pulsing certitude a gently
Wavering assurance. the sea throws
Silver coins at the rock. The whimbrel, that shuns
The sight of man, passes down the coast
And a heron follows, for if we are still
We are welcomed, if we are one we are met.

3.
A wind up the coast, scent of a milling nation
Traverses the brow so calm a bright
Disposal is for a fraction carved a bit
Above his hand and for a fraction the ever
Fractious lark curves over his head. He says I am but
A shepherd of the plain, without ambition, later dead.

4.

Stuck in the middle of life, that ungently
Grinds of ruin while the sea is a knife thrown
Across the earth. This evening it darkens
From grey to white and draws at what cost
I don't know the light from the fields until
Swathed in shade I let it go for sixpence net.

5.

My O my I thought I had a notion
To validate with truth this brittle
Spending, at every smile and every bite bent
Closer to the ground shifting the weather
Onto my back and wearing like Canute
A crown of clifftop grass and soil all the way to bed.

6.

Now it is the middle of night. The empty
Waves continue to knock on the land, down
There. Still some light clings to the sea and the floss
Flickers on the rocks. Human will bearing its star-crossed
Ensign haunts the black interior for good or ill. Spots
Of rain on my coat, are you with me yet ?

7.

And it will be good. The clouds open: a true equation
Dominates the eastern sky, bright Queen of it:
The shadow of the earth rises across the firmament,
Proving us truly here. And working hard, wherever
Some portion of true hope lies open in the cut
Of a single life, knife, wife, strife, head.

8.

When I get back to the caravan it is twenty
To four. Stumbling in the darkness I hear a moan
Of blame, a sleeping urge to die and quit this mess.
But there is no speed at all, no wily ghost.
I tuck the blankets round me heavy with dew,
Closing on sea moon and all, but alive in you.

Lines at the pool above St.-Saturnin

Alpine swift (the white chested) carving the air
And a quick wind from the hills redolent of
Pine and lavender rides the rocky cleft.
Skimming the surface our sight remains
Unpolitically tabulated / Innocent in delight
It is perfectly right, forswearing a life
Fixed in ratio to demand like a permanent
Insect-target for the flashing creature.
All we ask is that the heads of the town
Inscribe justice faithfully.

What do we know of world and detail who can't
Compete with the swift for vantage in the
Dream of earth? That speed of gain and grace
Leaves us standing, lost in our weight and
Hesitance, lost in delight at the fruitless sight
Of the species pilot fixing history to a dive.

But delight closes and light rises. The limbs
Tremble and bow to the mind that pokes
The blazing episphere of the day at its fault,
Facing world torsion with what? with a politeness,
A reasonable plea: *Raste Krieger, Krieg ist aus.**
Beautiful silent answers move over the hills.

So among ruined walls and broken arches
We forswear a hope that has no substance
Set sticks on bricks, gather truthful items from
The surrounding area and algebraize a sequence.

Later the lake dims, the birds retire,
The mind or something silently similar
Hovers in plagal trust in the crumbling air;
Talking to death at the ancient gate,
Where the locust passes, and the woody stalk.

"Hold it, soldier. War is out"

Lacoste

The landscape is a thought thing, it
Has been thought as a gift and as a burden.
We drive through someone's book to
The Marquis de Sade's castle, where misthought
Has left not a trace.

House prices flutter and electronic pastoral
Beats the air to no result: the true architecture
Speaks only *vulgare illustre*, heartstuff,
Dialect/reduction/vantage stand flat to the side,
Everything except justice is an impertinence.

It is a crowned structure, a hill
Rearing to intellect and lust as a burden
Patiently and proudly borne, set
Clear above the fruiting plain
Brighter stone than star because thought
                                        flawed

Recalling Lacoste

Back at night in a quiet room
Total country silence. Dim bulb
Moth at window, bread and cheese
Côtes du Rhone Beaumes de Venise 1985
Cheap but delicately heartening.
Silent tonight, reading a pocket
Guide or Dante and thinking of home.

The castle ringed the summit in white, the village
Houses were its skirts trailing into the ridged fields.
One does what one does of course, but only
What we know we do does much good.
The village dog barks twice and stops. Thin
Noise of someone's music. There is
A question always at hand, sometimes a horror,
Which we are entitled to neglect, with

Courtesy. And could do much
More but look at the time.

Up the Big Hill and Back By Ten

Walking the mind, walking the prosody,
Uphill, hour upon hour on a stone track
Through the garrigue and straight up the hot hill.
It is numbered. The little oaks whisper
The numbers are there whatever you do
Or say, no rests or interludes, sheer calm
Continuing as the numbers last, when
The numbers are full you are there. No one
In. A bright green lizard on a stone.

So we turn, descend, count on. A wasps' nest
Up a tree, a mantis' egg-sac under
A stone. Unkempt mountain lavender fields
Thyme, alkanet, early purple orchid
Remote farms up in the hills where much more
Than entire lives have been played out and love
Has been doubled or quartered and time clicks.

Politics is a play of fear. Fearful
Clicking of time in the hills as if a
Life is never enough meaning. It is
More than enough. A book in my pocket
By Dante, a pocket edition. When
We get back we'll have bread and cheese with wine
And count the day to its figured close.

S. Cecilia in Trastevere

What moves between bright thoughts and finished body?
Music's Idea turns in the clouds and She
Lies on the floor, denied her time, face
Turned away so as not to view her own pain...

What moves between is all we live, heavy
And light banked in winged tiers, that we
Carve our eyes through day to day, kiss
The bed and back to the devastating sight again...

I believe in a centre to the wasted life
That is carried before the world and holds love
Through distance and strife to the end of a
Perfect reconciliation however many times
Occluded in failed responses finally standing
Whole and obvious, like an orchard in the rain.

Little Bolehill

The stack of days is useless, there's nothing,
The days are nothing in the pocket no books
On the shelf: a white wall and a black kettle.
You can think & feel freely but there is nothing
Left of the day to have or write into a book
Or stack away, finally only a cup and a kettle
That we take with us into the garden where nothing
Grows except statues and ideas or sometimes books
But a real enough garden with leaves. Put the kettle
On the brick-lined hearth to simmer as the book
Says and pour slowly, hot water on the leaves.
Perhaps it is a life's richer act to wish nothing
Further than its own creation out of nothing
Of a real and final thing as true as leaves.

Meditations in the Fields

1.
Strolling in the olive groves and
Orchards, dry sky and hot stones,
Hard light and Ockeghem on the walkman —
I time the intervals. They are tightly numbered
And of such extent, such meeting parts

That all the time I wasted in disuse
(Bed, social time, infant fear)
And wasn't treading the mind's width
Is reckoned to my regret and returned
Untouched to the earth, or so it seems.

2.

Gazing at the ground
Wild thyme and sparse grass
The blue bellflower, Aphyllanthus
Monspeliensis, hanging over the stones
Between the cherry trees patches of sunlight
And Josquin in the earphone I
Am told out. We receive everything
And return it, in the flesh,
Now because it is charted. The flesh
Fruits so fulsome and glad precisely
As farmed, didn't they say?

3.

Pausing in the hot vine fields, Brumel
Through the wire seeming to say
That mutual enemies debate in the
Chambers of the heart, as Dante
Definitely said, and a small spirit
Pleads to the soul through a thin wire:
Regain your place. And sweet and low
(As thyme fills the air) O scouring focus
Neglect our substance if you will but
Shepherd this instant to its kingdom as only
The sharpened spirit kens and quickly —
Shew mercy on those good shepherd on
Us ourselves, the very ones who
Sit alone for their receipt in a foreign field
Send us to our remembrance, it's time
Clear enough through the crackle and fuzz
Death's silence leading each tone
Onwards, to lock the door
And fall into human length.

4.
Anywhere in the world the
Mind wakes while I
Contemplate a field corner and now
Lassus in the speaker telling
Of a rose entrammelled in the years,
Surviving as so much else
Continues to exist, so much
Pain and disappointment
The rose we make again, that you would
Never recognise or credit as that same
Armonia, that unfolding, clad in
The regency of the moment —
A silent and remote
Fold in the edge of the hills
Where a few things grow and I
Harvest exclusive result.

from *Alstonefield*

I

Again the figured curtain draws across the sky.
Daylight shrinks, clinging to the stone walls
and rows of graveyard tablets, the moon rising
over the tumbling peneplain donates some equity
to the charter and the day's accountant
stands among tombs, where courtesy dwells.
Thus a slight and special enclosure is set,
slight as the dark spaces I fill tonight and
silent and motionless as lives become, swelling
with truth, scattered with glowing plaques.

Darkness opens the sky to space. Fallen
light sets up its booth in the stoneyard
where the theatre of eyes flickers
and dies. The moon sails the sky, rides
the upland fields in sole possession, the
scattered runs of grey wall the walled yard

and the speaking stones, that say there is
something made in a life not to be lost
however small it is not to be crossed,
not to be cast in sightless wax.

But is kept folded in this unvalued space
space free of us where the moon slices time.
Void of us, where we didn't take any
advantage but sailed away, leaving
old bones kicked around the churchyard
and carried off by dogs and wrote out
the only true thing we are, a record
of love. Every impossible meeting
happens here in darkness and silence
and the slightness of the piecing mind.

A beautiful thing, the moon on stone, and
central. In a momentary breeze the trees
sway slightly and clap over the churchyard,
patches of hawthorn and yew claiming some
marginal light part towards the edge
leaving the moon's direct file on old names.
A refuge from the world that bears the world
and sets standards of dealing. How
could you secretise the language on this
final stage or place a reserve on hope

When the world is watching you? Mirror flashes
on the horizon, distances steeped in petrol,
lives snapped to zero across thronging waste and
drawing up lists of jews in Mansfield. Death
pressed through the dream into constant
separation as the waking world coats itself
in advantage, factorial of despair, that
defeats the bearer absolutely wall to wall:
the action without cause, the daylight caves.
We turn our backs, only the night is kind.

Of course we turn our backs, what is there
to speak through the coils of resentment
but denial, heart loss across the mirror

that coats the bank what is claimed but self?
I retire to a distance, I have the right
in the late evening and on through the dark hours
keeping to the edge of the necessary plot:
trade, marriage, maintenance, the sacred cast
of continuance always at risk, fixed with loss,
moon marks on stone, trenching the calendar.

I thought I heard in the still night air
a mother suckling her babe and singing
softly in the darkness: Poor little mite,
the cruel captains of earth will close
thy virtue to their lost standing in
spite, and all thy trust in good will
have to find its own way to the centre
without me, who am not there. Poor
accidental thing, she said, poor rabbit,
what ardour you bear to an unknown point.

Her milk was blue in the sky, it was
time to go. The moon like a knife in water
slid silently down the firmament and sank
into the trees and hedges, shaking themselves
in the dawn wind. The question frames
the response in emergent green: my life
may be kept in some spare cupboard as
needed from time to time or not but
the light spread again through the grass stalks
and the flesh trembled in its window.

I must be blind, to see such brightness
in such delicate light, to see the world
in its hope as a leaf turns in the
movement of cool air a memory trace
sufficient to keep a name in stone
the letters full of moss, I would serve
for ever the few ecstasies that form
such a purpose, the child's space at
the table, anger stretching into the future,
obedience glowing at every joint.

GAEL TURNBULL

from *A Winter Journey*

That hour —
hour of the wolf,
the hour to dawn —
    when only the hellebore is in flower
that hour —
    when every sweet is sickly,
    every freshness, sour
that hour—
    when you grip the battlements of an echoing tower
    and the stairs you have climbed have turned to salt
    beneath each step and fallen away and memory is a
    sunken shaft and all desire a stone that drops and
    there is no sound come back within the hour
that hour —
    when you're flung beyond the stars through a gap in
    time and are given every choice to choose and have
    no power
that hour —
    when every pride must fawn
    and even love must cower
that hour —
    when there are no lids to hide the dark
    that gropes behind your eyes, the silence
    that deafens every thought, the sense that numbs
    the very chance to feel, the hope that crushes,
    the emptiness that bloats, the stillness
    that intrudes, the weariness that shatters rest,
    the absence that won't let you be, the nothingness
    unwritten, staring, the blank pages turning
    that devour
that hour —
hour of the wolf,
the hour to dawn.

from *From the Language of the Heart*
Some Imitations from the Gaelic of Sine Reisideach

It Was

It was a good boat, never better
and the sailing—winds, tides, harbours,
storms, discoveries—beyond telling
but now past salvage, good only for the axe.
Don't flinch. Every splinter
familiar as your breath, the wreckage
soon dried out, ready for kindling
to burn steadily enough on the nearest headland,
a clear mark to be seen far astern,
on which to set a new bearing to steer
a new course with new companions
on a strange ship towards an unmarked horizon.

It Is Not

It is not the size of the peats
nor their number
nor anything particularly remarkable
about their shape or their quality
that sustains a fire

but it is their continued placing
without fuss and in due sequence
around the centre of the hearth
especially at morning and at night
so as not to starve or scatter or smother

thus it is with our affection

decide to put it out if you choose
but don't let it die
for lack of a little ordinary care.

from *Impellings*

As from a fleece, twisting together

where imperatives of wind disperse
the fall of leaves — and more
than half a century of rings are since
inscribed within those trees that shroud
stone lions sentinel above a roar
of cars — only grass renews unchanged
amid the litter by the railed off sundial
'silken as a dove's wing, time'
where first steps lifted forward

near that remembered haven, walled
and sunlit garden of my grandparents,
a sea mark shrouded far astern until,
at random past that door, found open,
with young couple and their infant son
just moving in, had sight again
down passage to that same unchanged
held place, made present and thus shed
to him and those unknown, come after me

according to the interval, according to the context

by shipyards and that venerable well
where history was compiled and I
first walked to school then later came
to stay with friends, midwinter festival,
by chance and choice, to call on one
whose resonance of words I knew,
thought dead or exiled, telling there
of his oldest friend, I never met, whose son
in time I did, to become thus mine

in the south where — at summer gathering
by resting place of one who shaped
from another tongue, fresh cadences — I met

the mother of that son, exiled, estranged,
from a former age who wrote of hills
where by vagrancies of time I came to walk
by another also venerated well
'found cold spring water...bathed my eyes...
had quite forgotten how far one might see'

take hold anywhere and all shall follow

'...who come, then go, and must
we know not from nor where...'
in words compiled of one who spoke
unmarked by name 'as bird
that flits from dark to dark
through hall in winter lit by flame
where men hold court... and know
only in mind of others do we stay,
are held to linger briefly, fade'

where they came once and built
in wood, not stone, a hall
between a river and steep hills
where you may also come, then go,
to stand alone in that almost
forgotten place, and find no trace
of mould or rubble, know how good
the silence, deep the air,
how sheer the meadow is, unmarked

one gulp of air is all we have

bees, honeysuckle, sound and scent
in the ruin of a mill house at Rhos Goch,
dust in my throat, a drifting afternoon,
remembering the day by day of one,
three generations past, recording tales
he heard repeated of the miller who

sleeping in the mill trough at midsummer
'often saw the fairies dancing
by moonlight' where I stood

and dust, soon harvest, hum of a car,
long roads through Périgord to Ribérac
where as a boy I had always longed to go,
then to laze in the square, amazed,
drinking a 'citron', scent and savour,
to be where he was born who made his songs
in an older tongue less spoken now,
transmuted yet by others, lingering
on other tongues, paced syllables

impelled by riches, not poverty

with a generation lapsed to the day
since 'given your address' you wrote
in soon familiar script, then came
at my reply, bring that 'Njala'
of 'bare style... more full' or 'glad
that you fell ill since it kept you
here' up the Gatineau where we walked
years afterwards in snow or along the Wye
with 'hard times also... mostly good

just hard to see sometimes just how'
or counterplying 'what no confessor
will ever hear us say... enjoyed
myself all the time that I was there'
who are moving now and yet remain
your self 'to a smaller house
eleven miles away' or near
'remembering the good times gone'
your hand 'and ever gone to stay'

articulate beyond mere sequence

imaged in words, as news from nowhere,
awakening to what might be, in a dream
of where a dustman 'while the sun
flashed back from him at every step
as if clad in golden armour' strolls
toward us on some casual morning
'with that somewhat haughty mien
great beauty is apt to give' to bring
discarded things to whatever lasting place

and from beyond the curve of the world
out of a storm of light and spray
Columba's boat steers to us and that island,
burial place of kings, who comes a stranger
to the land that he made his, claimed him,
watched by two lads, dumbfoundered,
sprawled on the machair— in the pigments
of that painting which still hangs
within a stroll of where I came to birth

in frequencies beyond prediction

listening to a retired prospector
near Hudson Bay—huddled by the stove
columned icicles from eaves to sill—remark
it was his uncle who had hired the coach
by which the famous rebel had escaped—thus
to pre-empt one side, placate the other,
maybe save confederation—with the money
and connivance of his opponent: which
is not a detail in the history books ·

and in the Mojave Desert, near high summer,
up some back canyon, engine flooding,
wouldn't run less than full throttle — so
nothing for it but to dismantle carburettor,
never done before, no manual, hardly guessing
even the problem, then reassemble, found:
obstruction in the needle valve — just one

brass shaving, hair thin, glittering, no more
than half length of a finger nail

granting momentum to each particular

where an ash tree reaches out
its branches with an eagle
its roots coiled with a serpent
and a squirrel runs between
to provoke, make variation
by shuttling motion, restless
as the unwearied flick
to keep a spindle turning
thread winding on a shaft

so the spiral chains reduplicate,
reshuffle origins, divide,
rejoin, each ply unwinding
propagates, transmits beginnings
with change as subtle, unremitting
as tracings in a patch of sand
inscribed afresh each day
by the shifting cycles
and cross currents of the tide

continuously transformed, always conserved

who was tormented by all he could not say
or do, among other things to gather
all the Titians, Tintorettos, Veroneses
into one great gallery of marble and serpentine
and get them all perfectly reproduced
so that everyone who wanted could have copies
and then go himself to draw all the subjects
of Turner's 19,000 sketches of Switzerland
and Italy and further elaborate or complete

and to get everyone in the world a dinner
who hadn't one and find out why they hadn't
and then hang all the knaves responsible,
not that he had any personal animosity
but it would be good for them and even better
for the world though sometimes he despaired
and just wanted to rearrange and relabel
his entire mineral collection or even
be perfectly quiet and not even think

down through the eye of the millstone

taken by a stroke three weeks later
which left him unable to speak or write
except for the occasional syllable —
impossible to understand in spite of effort —
otherwise lay, had bowels and bladder emptied,
squeezed her hand, took sips of liquid,
sometimes waved one arm at the ward
or opened his eyes and shook his fist
until heart and breath faded out

and at the crematorium in the middle
of several miles of derelict expanse,
there was a pile of rubbish lying outside
including floral sprays with violet ribbons
still wrapped in their plastic covers
abandoned from a previous funeral
that the wind suddenly tumbled across
the car park towards us and which no one
appeared to notice or find remarkable

exacting a means for, by contrivance

and outside the town where the camp had been
there is nothing to mark the place
except a tall stone, a plaque, a few words,

the dates and several acres in the forest
of harrowed and bleached earth where nothing
is allowed to grow, a place cared for
but not with love, that nothing
not the least blade of grass might ever
again be where such things had once been

and in a patch of neglected woodland
between farms, the undergrowth so thick
he could scarcely walk, after thirty years
where his comrades had died, buried
in unmarked graves, their enemies also,
fighting for three days without sleep
or food, for a few yards of ground, now
dense with brambles and wild blackcurrants
such as he had never seen, like grapes

through what we seek, what comes to hand

met, begging near Tollcross, no coat,
summer jacket 'grew up, children's homes'
on street now, four months 'sleep
where I can... bus shelters, doorways...
'until shifted on...' where the sheddings
of affluence are disposed by a wind
that slashes across the Meadows as if
direct from the stars, and where the mark
of each foot is dark against the frost

and on a shimmering screen: vagaries
of snowflakes on the wind, men cheering
at shipyard gates, with image of a man,
his tatar profile, crashing into rubble, who
'did nothing by halves' shifted history,
laughed once at irony, 'sat down to chess
unwillingly' and before dying spoke again
'somewhat sadly' of an old comrade from whom
he had, by much necessity, parted

who cling and yet relinquish

'we found him crawling along the track
who told how he met the other unexpectedly
both with guns at the ready, both had fired,
both fell, he wounded in the leg had hidden
behind a tree, tried to reload, but the ball
jammed half way, or would have fired again
at the son whom he watched dig a grave,
lay his father in with weapon and blanket
then cover with dirt and so get away...

...in a land very good to many poor people
with hunting and trapping, wild duck,
all kind of fish in the creeks and lakes,
berries, nuts, even vines in the woods
which we cleared bit by bit, at first
growing wheat and corn between the stumps
and after the rocky hillsides we came from,
the earth so rich, perhaps no wonder
that each wanted it for themselves'

in a propagation of waves

morning, already heat haze, watching
an Indian woman, Tumamait or Shamash,
down from the hills near Santa Ynez
within glitter of the Pacific surf —
the scorched air thick with scent
of anise, eucalyptus, sage —
her eyes, under tatar eyelids, dark
as wells without reflections, caverns
into a past and distance beyond us

and at dusk, blurred by falling snow,
five of them from off the tops,
largest of creatures in this land,
only a few paces from our door,

in winter coats, some still with antlers,
as in cave paintings, charcoaled, ruddy,
massive in shoulder, turning their great heads,
not cautious but aloof, part with the storm,
their eyes unseen upon us

gripping upon itself, compact of detail

the song patterns of many birds
'much too rapid in variation
for the human ear to distinguish'
and certain butterflies 'transparent scales
with opaque particles to scatter the light
creating the same blue as the sky overhead'
and under volcanic pressure and temperature
in the deepest rifts of the earth
'living organisms that thrive'

and by the shore of an open bay
watching the crests of the long rollers
from the full reach of the Atlantic
as they move in from over the horizon
in unwearied sequence to some rhythm
familiar beyond definition, to remember
the eyes of a man by the road somewhere
in the southern bush who said, when asked
how many years he'd lived, just 'much'

steering by where we come from

after day's travel, equatorial sun,
rinsing beneath a waterfall to glimpse
a rainbow there inside the shimmer
within a handsbreadth of our hands;
or again, toward Iona, sailing
south of Mull, between the squalls,
snow on our decks at Easter, the refraction

of three quite separate and concentric arcs
in company with him, my shipmate then

geologist, surveyor, traveller, who
through mountains on earth's farther side,
after day's toil, wandered some steps
to watch the sunset, slipped: three days
to reach the body, frozen at that height,
so heaped a cairn, in the Gilgit Valley
ringed by peaks, his resting place
in that dry air, such clarity and where
are no rainbows, who has need of none

CATHERINE WALSH

from _Idir Eatortha_

have you ever seen snow
and of course when the snow gets deep
some places say high up on the hills
have you ever played games in snow
lying deep to leave a shape
throwing snowballs rolling snowfolk
it's cold
there are lots of stories about snow

a Russian one

the wish
          divine
working hard at it hard at it

she's not a real girl
          but she's ours

                    the opposing currents

the wish
          divine

          or as rambling the frozen locks we went on teatrays
scraping by the lucky breadcrate owners every step beyond your
road's barrage of snowballs in the neck running
ducking running after them the nearest unmushed heap still
white on top away from feet tyres paws
          or digging digging out paths pavements sand here
salt there a grocery shop list hasty system distributing
scarce provisions
                    it got you moving
                    sequence of change
                    necessity

are you leaning to one side now
use the opposite arm to the leg
that's bending sweeping it right
up across the sky

                    have you ever seen snow

flakes falling

              spun out

    pane   still   winging   on

    belief

    that writes "time passes never to return to us
           and sorrow is then of no avail"

    quibble

                  [itchy toes]

by the sea   on the shingle
  shore   say

a long   or if
                  tide's out

boat
  time   net stretched

since   high
sailing   on the stones
              behind
  twice
or more

going there

        or as with toes
        protruding happily old

groynes goal posts

he draws heart trees sun
trees people trees

black sun on blue tree
petals   stuck out

                        tonight windy that
                        summer way leaves flap
                        wetly pavement toning
                        lighter

— ah the flagrant moment —

                    pale elongated
lengths   soft down
felt beneath   others
stencil foreheads   cresting   widow's
     peak
            — has it become one —

sleep cockatoo

          having trusted you
          trusting you

          — only —
or is it every one each so closely by all other

          mingling
      yet
not
      at all   all
   see
                        — still
                        nothing
                        happening *is*
                        don't ya know

to notice some quality of
   all ways   interminable

          almost
          redemption

       watch it!

                        suasion

techniques ego manufactured skill result
based achievement scale pattern self
deceit defeat

— I kept it alive —

a reasonable axis for all
   the I   survival
      necessity of inquiry
        wander and wonder
changing shadows round
   to get lost in

unlimited life   getting caught
   incomprehensible   in the reduction
                  of nothing

measuring time
   between   living things

   tight line

Nearly Nowhere

           layers of geological
           aggregates compacted
           in the slightest grain

the word I tried to remember to say to you

was saraband
it could have been anything
in the still of heat out of breath I would
fan you   lowered shades   I would fan
you if you were

700 years and 6
not a separatist
people great
uniformity manufactured
difference normal

abuse difference viewed as
     problematic   role defined
                         threat

                    divisive

use difference is
evolvement   role defining
                                   catalystic
                                   necessary factor
part of a whole socio-linguistic pattern

          our women's minds

egalitarian paper
ripostes

never easy watching faces
fall in but it works
they feel better
giving up briefly
the fight
torpor   languishment
isolate in the
    spectrum of

    prestige is a brand name too

vast patina   skimming the
convex tops shards of
glass
        hairline cracks
bicycling   stops

    wheeling over

    whee   leying   down

    the stair well

trenchcoat and turbine

    here
        I move

    to
    quit

acceptation

John Welch

The Shame of the Oracle

Darkness spawning light, night that begets the day,
shame that fractures the oracle's voice ...
*from **My Life** by Kamal Das*

1

Remembering forebears, to
    Fornicate in a grove
Under an awning of sunlight

Commensal again
    By a shallow lake in the forest
The outspread hand of the sky

Oak leaves float like letters
    On its barely perceptible surge
Leaf-mash below the surface makes

A metallic chestnut glitter.
    He has put on as armour
The brass plate of the sun

2

Their children collect sprouting
    Acorns in motorway-earshot
A voice travels out of a hollow

In such a miasma
    Soaking webs stretched across grasses
Small nets of water

Round them the leaves trickle down
    Graffiti cover the monument
They circle the grove read the signs

Gathering there in the dusk
    Geese feed on protected waters
The fisherman waits

For that mute thing to break the surface
    It will rise into consciousness
It will drown in revelation

The forest border's a wave
    That does not engulf the city
But disgorges riders and walkers at twilight

Into this liminal moment.
    The geese fly over the city
Slipping its halter of lights

3
Actaeon: transformer
    Who travels but gets no further
In the painted autumn wood

Down rainwet tracks
    A sudden crash of hooves
The water whipped up in shallow frenzy

It's dusk
    The rush hour traffic's piling up
Not knowing what pulls him back

Beside the glimmer of water
    He feels their hot breath closing
Flooded with the unequal gift

He assumes the mask again
    It's about not looking
He turns away to the choir

Of bird song trees in full leaf
    The flight orator grounded
And pulled down into the mire

4
What has been slaughtered in us
    Now rises into its origin
And moves in us again

Between the two worlds moving.
    The chalice of menstrual blood: envy
Possessed this gift

Who calls, who coils
    Something to move your heart
Less emptiness, more hope

Swallowing, coupling
    Giving birth, devouring
Dressing the vine with ash

November, and
    Withered by cold
The last chrysanthemums falter

Brought to an inner zone
    Its flayed sky, flakes of sunlight
Struck off the core

Hurrying to the Underground
    Whether the year opens or closes
Each clutching the badge of event

At dusk perhaps it begins
    Accompanied by some music
So much silence surrounds the music

'Pagoda
    Evenings in Granada
Gardens in the rain'

November sits in the park
    Beside the abandoned fountain
Where the leaves swirl and rattle

We are led across the sky
    Henceforth by an
Impersonation of the god

5

Spilt rose of blood
    Bright on the threshold
The virgin seal the icon choir

Such a scheme of silence
    Sings in there
'Fliessendes Wasser: Heil des Mundes'

Gender flow and substance
    Gesture: spillage
Thought coming in the mouth

Labials in earth and slime
    The sky comes down on it
And how this substance shines!

6

Alcohol singeing the brain-cells—
    The night will bring
Its wonders of hoof and horn

The fire in the head
    And the dead piling up:
Parents and dreams.

Sleep on in your house of blood
    Its feathered air, pulse of wings
As in a dream

The Egyptians have come into London
    Flutter of music blown on a stick
Video games by the terminus

And the British Museum like a temple
    Awash with traffic at dusk.
Inside 'Heh God of Millions'

'Four sons of Horus on a lotus flower
    The deceased and an ape adore the sun-disk
Water gods of eternity and the sea'

In here
    Sky-goddess is raised off the earth god's prick
By a god of the air:

*And Hunefer adoring Yesterday and Tomorrow, symbolized by the
two lions of the horizon:*

That Night

He wrote them all down, the missing
    Fathers so large with their absence
Their dates swimming into his head
    He went to the glass-fronted book case

And took out the piece of flayed cloth
    Its scorchings, incisions, her name
Where it hovered in the air
    He remembered the changing her body gave him

Such a plume of love
    Together nursing unacted desires
Smells of the karma-past. Together
    They forced open the door of light a little.

He looks out onto a fallen street
    Night coming down, in all its shades
Iron or rose in the sky
    That bitter glow not rightly understood

Now he takes down the book of lightnings
 Bound in its shrivelled integument
In the brace of the neck
 A throbbing pain, suppressed angers

'You and I, the skin of a dream—
 Tonight, on this soil of separation
We gaze into the face of love
 Whose child sleeps on unhindered

Night melts in their arrival, who bring
 Wonders, the serpent
Is caught by the throat, held in the shade
 Under the cover of sleep

Not the sun itself, rising, but the moment
 Of sunrise, this fist of light, sperm
Dries on its petals
 He who burns at the door, the name of the herald

This brindled stone of lightnings,
 Tablet of thunder, is born of becoming
How it rests here now in the palm
 Gently, it does not oscillate even.'

He goes upstairs
 Where his body falls back on the bed
November twilight, alcohol and flame
 They are taking the boat to exile

He opens the glass-fronted book case...

from **Its Radiance**

Something that doos not know us: but that we are known by

Its radiance
    sent part of you to sleep.
You woke beside this other.
Separately each breathes. Light rises, falls.

Hydrangea near the sea-shore's speckled pink.
Sunlight and wind comb the tamarisk over the rock
Whose turning edge will lift us into time—

A piece broke off and weathered.
We're in the gap that opens out,
Blood-berries, on a white sky.

Rain blowing in the wind, the track still dry.
The words are in a shallow grave
But we can hear the sea together.

Between us the stone set wandering
Disturb the grey chips and send them skimming
Wait for the sea to return.

Pebble, roof of the mouth
Is lonely as the salt
On its cold forehead.

There is another book, one we sit reading
All afternoon, beside the sealed-up well.
The silent trumpet-flowers. It's overcast and still.

On a day the ants take flight.
They're covering the path, a living veil.
If I were asked to name you what could I say?

Going back the way I came, eating the path up
Nightfall, dew and its million forms of stillness.
These bring me to the room of you, blood-wine.

Was it us or the words?
Sun glinting
On the glass-fronted bookcase
Striking between

We were halfway between
The life and the book
Neither real nor unreal
Dust suspended in sunlight

Puffed up as the pages
Closed. Then a flutter
Of leaflight above my desk.
The garden filled up with wings

In the gradation of afternoon
Striped with hours like the tiger
In the theatre of wrecked flowers
In water the branch reared back from...

I opened the door
The words got there first
Making it ready

A book that's been
Lifted up in my name

Poor

Mouth-hunger

    anger

go out and get some

And write some

Filling the space

The space that opens
in my solar plexus
Take it out new for you

Is this, a book of stairs I climb

Mouth on top of a sort of stem
Out in it
Alcohol afternoon misery

Sluiced with cold
Buckets of sunlight

But O to be just where I am
And comfortable in my skin
The light a sufficient bribe

A poor thing that you

Came across

A battered thing

Among the rubble

A distant stadium

Whispered its crowds

And the snake made of colours
Will welcome me into myself —
My all-attentive skin's
A page of hunger

Make do with what I know
Pure want   a closing down silence
It leaves the clear high
Singing undisturbed

Should maybe end
All in heap of fragments
Today is a sense of walking
Out into empty street and sky

And I liked it, walking
All through the blameless weather
As if all the things in the world, were
Imagination's unfinished spectacle

I am. the human. Let me haunt you.
Just here behind your shoulder
And I'll be seeing what comes towards us
Each vacant face awaiting occupation

So will a loving claw relax
So let it open
Mirror to which
I steer's blind light
Is somewhere else, you
Held me, there, and did not spill a drop

I, a poor fire
Parents being the ones
To whom I never spoke

Refusing everything as I was bound
I must confess I
Feel the words crumble in my mouth

Beside the path, a wolf
We each patrol our border
He is a mask, two small gold eyes
More elegant than any dog
Contact with humans blunts them
Can't you see? His dead patrol

That night I daresay all were blind
Till I became, the stranger
Until I walked out into air like this
Swarming breast. A city. Any one
Would do for walking in. I'd made
A complicated pact with silence.

Last night I dreamed about my father

Only he was a famous poet

There is just me in the crowd

And a smell of japonica apples

Where I sit in October sunlight

Drinking my coffee in the park

My name is

Appetite   I sing

Acknowledgements

To Guy Birchard for permission to reprint *Shriven, Scrying, Objet Trouvé, Triptych* and *Coup de lance* from Neckeverse (Galloping Dog Press, Newcastle-upon-Tyne, 1989); *Country Music, 29th Birthday Suite, Every face has its looks, Orientation* and *"Where we have never been is real "*. from *Birchard's Garage* (Pig Press, Durham, 1991). *Behind the Lines* was previously published in *Original Gravity* (Pig Press, Staple Diet series, 1995).

To Richard Caddel for permission to reprint two sections of *Fantasia in the English Choral Tradition* from *Uncertain Time* (Galloping Dog, Newcastle-upon-Tyne, 1990), and the remaining poems from *Larksong Signal* (Shearsman Books, Plymouth, 1997).

To David Chaloner for permission to reprint *Revisions* and *Rural Pursuits* from *Trans* (Galloping Dog, Newcastle-upon-Tyne, 1989); *Further Instructions* from *Where Once Was* (Poetical Histories, Cambridge, 1989); *Foreword, "At the time of your departure"* and *"Wherever you settle"* from *The Edge* (Equipage, Cambridge, 1993).

To Peter Dent for permission to reprint an excerpt from *Place to Place* (Stingy Artist Book Co., Weymouth, 1993), and *Naming Nothing* which appears here for the first time in its complete form. Parts were previously published in *Louis Zukofsky or Whoever Someone Else Thought He Was: a collection of responses to the work of Louis Zukofsky* (North and South, Twickenham & Wakefield, 1988).

To Andrew Duncan for permission to reprint *Almond Wind* and *The June Sun Cast as the Absent Lover* from *Knife Cuts the Water* (Poetical Histories, Cambridge, 1990); *Literacy* from *Cut Memories and False Commands* (Reality Studios, London, 1991). *At Cumae* first appeared in *Oasis* and *Wind and Wear in Aix-en-Provence* in *Shearsman.*

To Roy Fisher for permission to reprint four poems from *Poems 1955-1987* (Oxford University Press, 1988).

To Anvil Press Poetry for permission to reprint *The Fifth Elegy* and *Grave Goods: Lithuania c. 6000 BC* from *Lost and Found* by Harry Guest (Anvil, London, 1983), and *Barsoom, High Orchids, Two Interpretations of a Piece by Grieg* and *The Sorcerer's Squares* from *Coming to Terms* by Harry Guest (Anvil, London, 1994). To Harry Guest for permission to reprint *A Very English Art* which previously appeared in *Slow Dancer.*

To Lee Harwood for permission to reprint *Coat of Arms on Wall in Ancient City* and *The Unfinished Opera* from *Rope Boy to the Rescue* (North and South, Twickenham & Wakefield, 1988); *Brecon Cathedral, On the Ledge* and *Cwm Uchaf* from *In the Mists* (Slow Dancer, Nottingham, 1992).

To Philip Jenkins for permission to reprint the complete text of *Cairo* (Editions Grand Hotel de Palme à Palermo, London, 1981).

To Grace Lake for permission to reprint poems from *Viola Tricolor* (Equipage, Cambridge, 1993), *Bernache Nonnette* (Equipage, 1995) and *Tondo Aquatigue* (Equipage, 1997).

To Tom Lowenstein for permission to reprint *La Tempestà's X-Ray* from *Filibustering in Samsara* (The Many Press, London, 1987).

To Christopher Middleton for permission to print the poems included here.

To David Miller for permission to reprint *Background Music* from *Pictures of Mercy* (Stride, Exeter, 1991), and *A path a lake the very breath, Confrontation* and *Landscape* from *Elegy* (Oasis Books, 1996). *Children* previously appeared in *tel-let* (Charleston, Ill.).

To Billy Mills for permission to reprint two sections from *Letters from Barcelona* (Dedalus Editions, Dublin, 1990), *reading Lorine Niedecker* and *"the stony field"* from *Five Easy Pieces* (Shearsman Books, Plymouth, 1997).

To Peter Riley for permission to reprint *Lines at the Pool above St Saturnin, Meditations in the*

Fields, Lacoste, Recalling Lacoste, Up the Hill and Back By Ten from *Noon Province et autres poèmes* (second (revised & bilingual) edition, Atelier La Feugraie, Saint-Pierre-la-Vieille, France, 1996); *Egbert Street* and *Golden Slumbers* from *Reader* (publisher not listed, London, 1992); *Section VIII, Seawatch* from *Seawatches* (Prest Roots Press, Kenilworth, 1991) and the Section I of *Alstonefield* (Oasis Books / Shearsman Books, London & Plymouth, 1995). *S. Cecilia in Trastevere* and *Little Bolehill* are reprinted from *Snow Has Settled [...] Bury Me Here* (Shearsman Books, Pymouth, 1997).

To Gael Turnbull for permission to reprint two poems from *From the Language of the Heart* (Gnomon Press, Frankfort, Ky, 1985), a section from *A Winter Journey* (Pig Press, Durham, 1988), and an excerpt from *Impellings*, published in *For Whose Delight* (Mariscat Press, Glasgow, 1995).

To Catherine Walsh for permission to reprint the final pages of *Idir Eatortha* from *Idir Eatortha and Making Tents* (Invisible Books, London, 1996).

To John Welch for permission to reprint *The Shame of the Oracle* from *Blood and Dreams* (Reality Studios, London, 1991; 2nd edition 1992), a section from *Its Radiance* and the sequence *Poor*, published in *from Greeting Want* (Infernal Methods, 1996).

Bibliography

Guy Birchard: *Neckeverse* (Galloping Dog, Newcastle-upon-Tyne, 1989), *Birchard's Garage* (Pig Press, Durham, 1991), *Memoirs of a Yohawk* (tel-let, Charleston, IL, 1996).

Richard Caddel: *Sweet Cicely: New & Selected Poems* (Taxus Press, Durham, 1983; 2nd edition, Galloping Dog, Newcastle-upon-Tyne,1988), *Uncertain Time* (Galloping Dog, 1990), *Larksong Signal: Poems 1990-1995* (Shearsman Books, Plymouth, 1997)

David Chaloner: *dark pages / slow turns / brief salves* (Ferry Press, London, 1969), *Year of Meteors* (Arc Publications, Todmorden, 1972), *Chocolate Sauce* (Ferry, 1973), *Today Backwards* (The Many Press, London, 1977), *Projections* (Burning Deck, Providence, RI, 1977), *Fading into Brilliance* (Oasis Books, London, 1978), *Hotel Zingo* (Grosseteste, Wirksworth & Leeds, 1981), *Trans* (Galloping Dog, 1989), *Where Once Was* (Poetical Histories, Cambridge, 1989), *The Edge* (Equipage, Cambridge, 1993).

Peter Dent: *Proxima Centauri* (Agenda Editions, London, 1972), *Focus Germanus: Episodes* (Oasis Books, London, 1978), *Distant Lamps* (Hippopotamus Press, Sutton, 1980), *From the Flow* (Taxus, Durham, 1983), *Uncloudy Wine* (Taxus, Leicester, 1987), *Midwinter Nights* (Oasis, 1988), *Night Winds and Dice* (Big Little Poem Books, Grimsby, 1990), *Suggesting Blue* (Room Press, White Plains, NY, 1991), *Northwoods* (Taxus, Exeter, 1992), *Place to Place* (Stingy Artist Book Co., Weymouth, 1993), *Equinox* (Oasis Books, 1993). As editor: *The Full Note: Lorine Niedecker* (Interim Press, Budleigh Salterton, 1983), *Not Comforts / But Vision: Essays on George Oppen* (Interim, 1985).

Andrew Duncan: *In a German Hotel* (Ochre, 1978), *Knife Cuts the Water* (Poetical Histories, Cambridge, 1990), *Cut Memories and False Commands* (Reality Studios, London, 1991), *From the Kitchen Floor* (Microbrigade, London, 1992), *Sound Surface* (Wiwaxia, London, 1992), *Alien Skies* (Equipage, 1993), *Pauper Estate* (Spineless Press, Plymouth, 1997).

Roy Fisher: *The Cut Pages* (Oasis Books / Shearsman Books, London & Plymouth, 1985), *Poems 1955-1987* (OUP, 1988), *A Furnace* (OUP, 1988), *Birmingham River* (OUP, 1994), *It Follows That* (Pig Press, 1994), *The Dow Low Drop — New and Selected Poems* (Bloodaxe Books, Newcastle upon Tyne, 1996).

Harry Guest: (all Anvil Press Poetry, London, unless otherwise stated): *Arrangements* (1969), *The Cutting Room* (1970), *A House Against the Night* (1976), *Lost and Found* (1983), *The Emperor* *of Outer Space* (Pig Press, Durham, 1983), *Coming to Terms* (1994). Novels: *Days* (1978), *Lost Pictures* (Albertine Press, Exeter, 1991). As editor: *Post-War Japanese Poetry* (Penguin, 1972), *Traveller's Literary Companion to Japan* (In Print, Brighton, 1994 & Passport, Chicago, 1995).

Lee Harwood: *The White Room* (Fulcrum Press, London, 1968), *Landscapes* (Fulcrum, 1969, *The Sinking Colony* (Fulcrum, 1970), *HMS Little Fox* (Oasis Books, London, 1975), *Boston, Brighton* (Oasis, 1977), *All the Wrong Notes* (Pig Press, Durham, 1982), *Monster Masks* (Pig, 1985), *Dream Quilt* (Slow Dancer, Nottingham, 1985), *Crossing the Frozen River: Selected Poems* (Paladin, London, 1988), *Rope Boy to the Rescue* (North & South, Twickenham & Wakefield, 1988), *In the Mists* (Slow Dancer, Nottingham, 1992).

Philip Jenkins: *On the Beach with Eugène Boudin* (Transgravity Press, Deal, 1978), *Cairo* (Editions Grand Hotel de Palme à Palermo, London, 1981).

Grace Lake: *La Facciata* (Poetical Histories, Cambridge, 1989), *Viola Tricolor* (Equipage, Cambridge, 1993), *Bernache Nonnette* (Equipage, 1995), *Parasol One. Parasol Two. Parasol Avenue*. (involution, Cambridge, 1996).

Tom Lowenstein: *The Death of Mrs Owl* (Anvil, 1977), *Filibustering in Samsara* (The Many Press, London, 1987), *Filibustering in Samsara - A Footnote* (Poetical Histories, 1990), *The Things that We Said of Them: Shaman Stories and Oral Histories of the Tikigaq People* (University of California Press / Douglas & MacIntyre, 1992), *Ancient land: Sacred Whale — The Inuit Hunt and Its Rituals* (Bloomsbury, London, 1993).

Christopher Middleton: (all Carcanet, Manchester, unless otherwise specified) *Torse 3* (Longmans, Green & Co, London, 1962), *Nonsequences / Selfpoems* (Longmans, 1965), *Our Flowers and Nice Bones* (Fulcrum Press, London, 1969), *The Lonely Suppers of W.V. Balloon* (1975), *Pataxanadu* (1977), *Carminalenia* (1980), *111 Poems* (1983), *Serpentine* (Oasis Books, London, 1985), *Two Horse Wagon Going By* (1986), *Selected Writings* (Paladin, London, 1990), *The Balcony Tree* (1992), *Some Dogs* (Enitharmon Press, 1993), *Floating Miniatures* (Sal Volatile Press, Austin, Texas, 1995). *Intimate Chronicles* (1996). Criticism: *Bolshevism in Art & other expository writings* (1978), *The Pursuit of the Kingfisher* (1983).

David Miller: *The Caryatids* (Enitharmon Press, London, 1975), *The Story* (Arc, Todmorden, 1976), *Primavera* (Burning Deck, Providence, RI, 1979), *In the Midst* (Stingy Artist, Alverstoke, 1979), *Losing to Compassion* (Origin Press, Kyoto, 1985), *Darkness Enfolding* (Stride, Exeter, 1989), *Pictures of Mercy: Selected Poems* (Stride, 1991), *True Points* (Spectacular Diseases, Peterborough, 1992), *Tesserae* (Stride, 1993), *The Book of the Spoonmaker* (Markings/Cloud, Newcastle-upon-Tyne, 1995), *Stromata* (Burning Deck, 1995), *Elegy* (Oasis Books, London, 1996), *Collected Poems* (University of Salzburg Press, Salzburg, 1997), *The Water of Marah* (Sun & Moon Press, Los Angeles, CA, 1997).

Billy Mills: *Genesis and home* (hardPressed Poetry, Dublin, 1985), *Triple Helix* (hardPressed, 1987), *Letters from Barcelona* (Dedalus Press, Dublin, 1990), *The Properties of Stone* (Writers Forum, London, 1996), *Five Easy Pieces* (Shearsman Books, Plymouth, 1997).

Peter Riley: *Love Strife Machine* (Ferry Press, London, 1969), *The Linear Journal* (Grosseteste, Pensnett, 1973), *The Musicians, The Instruments* (The Many Press, London, 1978), *Preparations* (Curiously Strong, London, 1979), *Lines on the Liver* (Ferry, 1981), *Tracks and Mineshafts* and *Two Essays* (both Grosseteste, Matlock, 1983), *Noon Province* (Poetical Histories, Cambridge, 1989), *Sea Watches* (Prest Roots Press, Kenilworth, 1991), *Reader* (London, 1992), *Sea Watch Elegies* (Poetical Histories, 1993), *Lecture* (Equipage, Cambridge, 1993), *Company Week* (Compatible, London, 1994), *Distant Points* (Reality Street Editions, London, 1995), *Alstonefield* (Oasis Books / Shearsman Books, London & Plymouth, 1995), *Royal Signals* (Short Run Press, Cheltenham, 1995), *Small Square Plots* (Grille, 1996), *Between Harbours* (Cambridge, 1996), *Noon Province et autres poèmes* (revised, bilingual edition, Atelier La Feugraie, Saint-Pierre-la-Vieille, 1996), *Snow Has Settled [...] Bury e Here* (Shearsman Books, Plymouth, 1997).

Gael Turnbull: *A Gathering of Poems 1950-1980* (Anvil Press Poetry, London, 1983), *A Year and a Day* (Mariscat Press, Glasgow, 1985), *A Winter Journey* (Pig Press, Durham, 1987), *While Breath Persists: New & Selected Poems* (Porcupine's Quill, Erin, Ont., 1992), *For Whose Delight* (Mariscat, 1995).

Catherine Walsh: *Making Tents* (hardPressed Poetry, Dublin, 1987), *Short Stories* (North & South, Twickenham & Wakefield, 1990), *Pitch* (Pig Press, Durham, 1994), *Idir Eatortha and Making Tents* (Invisible Books, London, 1996).

John Welch: *Six of Five* (The Many Press, London, 1975), *And Ada Ann* (Great Works Editions, Bishops Stortford, 1978), *Out Walking* (Anvil, 1984), *Blood and Dreams* (Reality Studios, London, 1991), *Erasures* (The Many Press, 1992), *Its Radiance* (Poetical Histories, 1993), *Greeting Want* (Infernal Methods, London, 1996).

WAR REPORT

In the last decade as a result of war

**2 million children have died,
5 million have been forced into refugee camps,
12 million have been left homeless.**

Children's Aid Direct has created an original drama presentation to highlight its campaign 'Children In War'.

'War Report' includes:

- details of how war affects children
- personal accounts from children
- details re the appalling rise in the number of children involved
- a positive message about what can be done.

If you would like to order a copy of 'War Report' or would like more information about Children's Aid Direct, please contact:

Community Support Team, Children's Aid Direct,
82 Caversham Road, Reading RG1 8AE
Tel: 0118 958 4000   Fax: 0118 958 8988
Web site: http://www.cad.org.uk
Email:enquiries%cad@notesgw.compuserve.com
Registered Charity No. 803236

Children's Aid *Direct*